OUR STORIES II

The Experiences of Black Professionals on Predominantly White Campuses

Edited by
Dr. Sherwood Smith
and
Dr. Mordean Taylor-Archer

JD●TT

*The John D. O'Bryant National Think Tank for Black Professionals
in Higher Education on Predominantly White Campuses
Cincinnati, Ohio*

Our Stories II: The Experiences of Black Professionals on Predominantly White Campuses
Copyright © 2006
ISBN: 0-9718888-1-7

published by:	The John D. O'Bryant National Think Tank for Black Professionals in Higher Education on Predominantly White Campuses
	University of Cincinnati, Contract Station
	P.O. Box 219097, Cincinnati, Ohio 45221-1097
	http://www.johndobryant.org
edited by:	Dr. Sherwood Smith and Dr. Mordean Taylor-Archer
composition by:	DPS Associates, Inc.
internal design by:	Daniel Van, DPS Associates, Inc.
cover design by:	Erv Swillinger, DPS Associates, Inc.
printed by:	King Printing Company, Inc.

ALL RIGHTS RESERVED
No part of this work covered by the copyright hereon may be reproduced or used in any form or by any means—graphic, electronic, or mechanical, including photocopying, recording, taping, Web distribution or information storage and retrieval systems—without the written permission of the publisher.

Printed in the United States of America
1 2 3 4 5 10 09 08 07 06

Library of Congress Control Number: 2006927106

The JDOTT book emblem symbolizes the everlasting rippling effect of love that was exhibited by the late John D. O'Bryant. His spirit continues to assist in the transformation of so many lives and is still only a stone's throw away.

This book is dedicated to the memory
of
John D. O'Bryant

A compassionate man who loved people;
Unpretentious, never flaunting his status or influence;
Always optimistic and reminding others
To keep things in perspective;
A man of great integrity who never judged others;
A spiritual man who practiced his Christian beliefs;
An educator who believed that our mission
Is to serve students.

(Northeastern University—Memorial Service—May 1, 1993)

Contents

Dedication iii
Foreword v
Acknowledgement vi
Introduction vii

Part 1: Personal Journeys within the System
The Phoenix Rising
      Sherryl N. Weston 2
African-American Studies Majors
      Nancy J. Nelson 12
Muses of a Mentor: A Tribute to the Elders
      Roland B. Smith, Jr. 20

Part 2: Stories from Graduate School, My Gender and My Race
Diary of a Superwoman
      LaTashia R. Reedus 32
From Disappointment to Purpose
      Terri M. Hurdle 42
On the Road to Success
      Ryan J. Davis 52
Just Do It—I Did It
      Juliana M. Mosley Anderson 74

Part 3: Teaching and Learning, Challenge and Support
Culture Shock in the Heartland
      Be Stoney 84
Giving All, Getting Half
      Jean Moule 94

Part 4: Outsiders within Our Organizations
Reflections on a Decade of Great Expectations
      Joyce Simons 106
1 Day and 3 Hours
      Nell Lewis 114
Alone and Assailed in the Heartland of America
      Stephen K. Appiah-Padi 122
Know Your Place or No You May Not
      Pam Mitchell-Crump 130
Epilogue 141

Foreword

The major conclusions of a number of recent studies analyzing the diversification of higher education over the last 20 years have found that the incremental progress achieved thus far is not occurring quickly enough. In fact, since the recent notable Michigan decisions (*Gratz v. Bollinger* and *Grutter v. Bollinger*), diversity in higher education may be getting worse. Poignant changes in affirmative action policies and practices have already eroded many of the meager gains achieved during the last 20 years. Continuing efforts by entities outside of higher education to challenge university affirmative action plans have effectively weakened diversity efforts on many predominantly white campuses. The actions of these groups represent societal attitude shifts that have also exacerbated an already dire situation.

Despite obstacles presented by these challenges, many black professionals continue to devise programs and policies that enhance their capacity to achieve effective change and maintain the relevancy of diversity. Volume Two of *Our Stories: The Experiences of Black Professionals on Predominantly White Campuses* chronicles the stories of black administrators and faculty who are on the frontlines of the struggle to ensure that blacks are aptly represented in all levels of this nation's institutions of higher learning.

Once again, the John D. O'Bryant National Think Tank for Black Professionals in Higher Education on Predominantly White Campuses has assembled a distinguished group of black professionals to tell their respective stories about life as faculty and administrators working at these institutions. This collection of black administrators and faculty, hail from a variety of U.S. colleges and universities and come together to share stories of their own professional higher educational experiences and to provide insights as to how they maintained their integrity all while facing overwhelming pressures.

Each personalized essay is reflective of a magnificent weaving of history with real-world events and provides fascinating details of not only the trials and tribulations but the success stories—lessons of these black faculty and administrators—as they confronted the many barriers that worked to impede progress in their heartfelt desire to achieve the goal of institutionalizing diversity.

Our Stories is a tribute to the success of these authors who have proudly stood upon the shoulders of the courageous ancestors and mentors that paved the way for their professional and personal opportunities, their wisdom, and their enduring values, as well as ethical convictions that can enhance us all.

Dr. Kenneth B. Durgans, President

Acknowledgments

Any book is the product of the efforts of many people. This is the case with *Our Stories II*, and we wish to express our appreciation to all those who supported this project. Our gratitude first goes to the Creator for making this book possible. Also, we want to acknowledge our ancestors who paved the way through unbearable oppression for us to be where we are today. A special acknowledgement goes to the late John D. O'Bryant, who had the vision to establish a national organization for black professionals in higher education on predominantly white campuses.

A special thanks goes to Dr. Ken Durgans and Dr. Eric Abercrumbie, whose vision for this book and whose persistence kept us on task. A heartfelt thank you goes to the authors who were willing to put in the blood, sweat, and tears to write about their experiences in ways that can be beneficial to others. A deep and sincere thank you for sharing so profoundly your struggles and triumphs in your life experiences on predominantly white campuses. A thank you to my staff, Mary Heininger, Tyler Branner, and Leigh Brannon for their support with this book project. And finally, JDOTT would like to acknowledge DPS Associates, Inc., especially Crystal Bullen, for their guidance and service in publishing our book

Introduction

It has been four years since we first presented *Our Stories* to the public at the National Conference on Race and Ethnicity in May 2002. In producing a *Our Stories II* we seek to accomplish two things. First, we want to continue on the journey of the African-American odyssey of higher education in the United States. Second, we wish to continue to validate the black lived experiences in all of its richness and contrast, joy and sorrow, frustration and elation.

This book is a challenge to the idea that prejudice, discrimination, and racism are things of the past (Monk, 2000). It gives voice to a reality which, if left unspoken, would support the fiction of the objectivity of the academy.

> "We must always take sides. Neutrality helps the oppressor, never the victim. Silence encourages the tormentor, never the tormented."
>
> Elie Weisel, Acceptance Speech, Nobel Peace Prize,
> New York Times, December 11, 1986

> "Because if I am not what I've been told I am, then it means that you're not what you thought you were either. And that is the crisis."
>
> James Baldwin, A Talk to Teachers,
> Saturday Review, December 21, 1963

Predominantly white institutions of higher education purport to value diversity and seek ways to increase the number of faculty, staff, and students of color on their campus (Otuya, 1994 and Neufedt, 1990). However, when asked about the low numbers, many colleges and universities give the disingenuous excuse of the difficulty in finding black faculty (Carter, D., 1993), the lack of competitive salaries (Cose, 1993), and their institutions inability to stop the revolving door and so retain those admitted or hired (Sutherland, 1990). The two most complex and inflexible issues of campus climate and institutional culture (Sheared, 1994, Spring, 2004, and Tatum, 1997) are often not addressed. Rarely have these predominantly white institutions'

Introduction ix

majority made efforts to understand the perspectives and complexities of black professionals' existence in their institutions or their part in constructing the environment (Gregory, 1999, Smith, 1995, Sutherland, 1990 and Thendeka, 1999).

This second *Our Stories* book contains more of the riveting and compelling experiences of black professionals on predominantly white campuses. The writers represent a cross-section of black professionals and students in various positions at colleges and universities across the United States. Each story gives the reader insight into the struggles, challenges, and triumphs that blacks have experienced (Collins, 2000, Shipler, 1999, and Smith, 1995). *Our Stories II* presents the authentic voices of those who not only have succeeded despite the odds, but who continue to make a positive difference in their institutions and in the lives of the students that they nurture, mentor, teach, and serve (Bell, 1992 and Perna, 2000).

The personal and professional journeys of these black men and women writers will provide the readers with sustenance as articulated in "The Phoenix Rising." Other stories are emotionally charged testimony to costs of prejudice and isolation, such as "African-American Studies Majors," "Giving All, Getting Half," and "Know Your Place or No You May Not." Some of the stories provide an understanding of the complex connection of family, friends, and institutional climate that shape our lives, such as "On the Road to Success," "Culture Shock in the Heartland," and "From Disappointment to Purpose." Others share how the struggle for social justice of the past still continues today, revealed in "Muses of a Mentor: A Tribute to the Elders," "1 Day and 3 Hours," and "Alone and Assailed in the Heartland of America." Some inspirational stories are grounded in the experiences of black women's spirituality and determination, as found in "Just Do It—I Did It," "Reflections on a Decade of Great Expectations," and "Dairy of a Superwoman."

This book represents both the personal stories of individual African-American faculty, staff, and students and their critical analysis aimed at providing a clearer understanding of the institutional and structural systems of racism (Shipler, 1999) and oppression within institutions of higher education (Bell, 1992, Gregory, 1999, and Spring, 2004). Overall, the stories provide individual strategies for success. This second book continues the JDOTT tradition of sharing personal experiences to make plain the larger struggles and achievements of a people. This work is another step in fulfilling JDOTT's mission to disseminate information and exchange ideas for the betterment of our students and our personal and professional lives.

Stories are grouped by themes and are arranged in a progression. The conscious intention from the progression of these stories is aimed at moving the reader from the personal context of individuals' journeys through authors' lives to an understanding of subtle prejudice at the institutional and structural levels that challenges them on a daily basis. The book gives real life examples of how challenges, obstacles, and success were dealt with at the personal level.

Part 1 gives readers insight into personal strategies for survival and success. We begin with three personal journeys:

The Phoenix Rising
This is the story of a first generation college student, administrator, and leader. We are given insight into the joys, fears, challenges, and achievement in her experiences of higher education. It is a view of the work to make change and suggestion of how to make the journey less stressful.

African-American Studies Majors
We are given a view into the life of students studying their own history. The story frames, in a clear light, the central issues of how new knowledge can be a painful gift in the predominantly white environment of higher education. It reminds us of the importance of sensitivity and compassion and the psychological pain of racism.

Muses of a Mentor: A Tribute to the Elders
This story frames the meaning of education through the lens of two major life events. We see the importance of social action and the pressures it places upon students. The story helps the readers understand how meaning is constructed through the impact of campus events on a student's life.

But the challenges are not just personal ones. There are professional challenges to be faced. Authors describe in detail the particular challenges presented to them in their careers. In Part 2 we present their success to remind us that it is difficult but possible, and to highlight some of the obstacles that we all should be aware of.

Dairy of a Superwoman
This is a personal story about the complexities an African-American woman faces in higher education. It is not just facing overt and conscious forms of bias; rather, this story exposes the variety of unquestioned privileges given to some and denied to others.

From Disappointment to Purpose
This is a life story. The author shares the fullness of her experiences over the full breadth of the educational system. This is a story of how a person makes the important choices in life and overcomes the challenges presented on the journey.

On the Road to Success: Helping Low-Performing African-American Male Undergraduates Become High Achievers
The reader is given insight into significant and personal experiences of an African-American male student. In addition, the story clearly shows the multiple factors that come together to nurture us as lifelong learners and university students.

Just Do It—I Did It
Here is a personal narrative that explores a personal journey through a graduate degree program. It describes the obstacles, hurdles, and roadblocks, as well as the mentoring and coaching that happen along the way.

Ultimately, racism and oppression are not just actions of individual prejudice but are examples of a systemic illness within our society. They are part of larger systems of bias. One of the writers' goals for us is to probe beyond individual experience. The intent is to enrich our understanding of the interlocking systems at work that attempt to marginalize African Americans at predominantly white institutions of higher education. Part 3 focuses on critically analyzing the larger institutional culture and creating responses that both challenge injustice and maintain our wholeness as human beings.

Culture Shock in the Heartland
The philosophy in this story is to learn and adapt. This story explores the experiences of a black faculty member as she handles both the personal and professional conflicts that arise from bias within higher education.

Giving All, Getting Half
This is a story of one African-American faculty making her way through white higher education. It will open the readers' eyes to the real world experiences and provides suggestions for handling situations and maintaining a social action focus.

The stories in Part 4 are grouped by themes and are arranged in a progression ending with a set of stories documenting success. At times, we as black professionals in higher education are the outsiders within our organizations. We are the "faces at the bottom of the well," and it is a well that many drink from without refilling (Bell, 1992). This can be a position of both unique opportunity (Neufedt, 1990) and painful isolation (Spring, 2004). We are required to perform a high-wire act in which we walk and sometimes run while juggling personal and professional selves balanced on the lines of insecure messages of commitment, support, and understanding. This part gives readers insight into personal strategies for success. We end *Our Stories II* with four different stories of outsiders' accomplishments.

Reflections on a Decade of Great Expectations
The relationship between the campus and the local community is critical to the success and well being of people of color. This is a story of coming together rather than maintaining the "town and gown" divisions that limit us both personally and professionally.

1 Day and 3 Hours
Events can shape our lives, and in this story the reader learns how important the responses to an event can be, especially when events can seem to be beyond our control. It is a story of challenge, resiliency, spirituality, and survival.

Alone and Assailed in the Heartland of America
There are many different parts to our lives. This is a story of the challenges in one's professional life. It helps us to understand the importance of the indirect, obtuse, and recalcitrant form that the political and institutional power and privilege.

Know Your Place or No You May Not
What to do? It's a question addressed throughout these stories. The intersections of gender and race, personal and professional, or simply marginalization are critically analyzed. This story closes this edition with specific suggestions for actions that can help us to succeed.

Throughout the book, *Our Stories II* has something for everyone. It is intellectual, spiritual, emotional, and insightful. Similar to John D. O'Bryant's life, the impact of this book and these stories will have far-reaching impact and significance in years to come.

Editors: Sherwood E. Smith, Ed.D.
Mordean Taylor-Archer, Ph.D.

References

Aguirre, Jr., A., "The Status of Minority Faculty in Academe," *Equity and Excellence in Education* 28(1) (1995), 63–68.

Carter, D. and Eileen, O., "Employment and Hiring Patterns of Faculty of Color," *American Council on Education Research Briefs.* 4(6) (1993).

Bell, D., *Faces at the Bottom of the Well: The Permanence of Racism* (New York: Basic Books, 1992).

Collins, P., *Black Feminist Thought: Knowledge, Consciousness and the Politics of Empowerment* (New York: Routledge, 2000).

Cose, E., *The Rage of a Privileged Class* (New York: Harper-Collins, 1993).

Gregory, S. T., *Black Women in the Academy: The Secrets to Success and Achievement* (Lanham, MD: University Press of America, 1999).

Maher, F. A., *Learning in the Dark: How Assumptions of Whiteness Shape Classroom Knowledge* (Harvard Educational Review. 67(2) (1997), 321-349.

Monk, R. C., *Taking Sides: Clashing Views on Controversial Issues in Race and Ethnicity* (Guilford, CT: McGraw-Hill, 2000).

Neufedt, H. & McGee, L., *Education of the African-American Adult: A Historical Overview* (New York: Greenwood Press, 1990).

Otuya, E., "African Americans in Higher Education," *American Council on Education Research Briefs* 5(3) (1994).

Perna, L., "Differences in the Decision to Attend College among African Americans, Hispanics and Whites," *Journal of Higher Education* 71(2) (2000).

Sheared, V., "Giving Voice: an Inclusive Model of Instruction—A Womanist Perspective." In E. Hayes and S.A.J. Colin III (Eds.), *Confronting Racism and Sexism* (San Francisco: Jossey-Bass, 1994), 27–37.

Shipler, D., "Subtle vs. Overt Racism." In V. Cyrus. (Ed.), *Experiencing Race, Class and Gender in the United States.* (Mountain View, CA: Mayfield Press, 1999).

Smith, S., *The Experience of African-American Faculty in Adult Education Graduate Program* (Ball State University, Muncie, IN. unpublished dissertation, 1995).

Spring, J., *Deculturalization and the Struggle for Equality: A Brief History of the Education of Dominated Cultures in the United States* (New York: McGraw-Hill, 2004).

Sutherland, M., "Black Faculty in White Academia: The Fit Is an Uneasy One," *Western Journal of Black Studies* 14 (Winter 1990), 17–23.

Tatum, Beverly Daniel, *Why Are the Black Kids Sitting Together in the Cafeteria and Other Conversations About Race* (New York: Basic Books, 1997).

Thandeka, *Learning to Be White: Money, Race and God in America* (New York: The Continuum, 1999).

Part 1

Personal Journeys within the System

The Phoenix Rising — Sherryl N. Weston

African-American Studies Majors — Nancy J. Nelson

Muses of a Mentor: A Tribute to the Elders — Roland B. Smith, Jr.

Sherryl N. Weston

Sherryl N. Weston is the owner and lead trainer of Westcloud Consulting (www.westcloud.org), a multicultural consultant and training services organization based in Denver, Colorado. Her workshops are focused on issues that relate to the shifting demographics in the United States, such as the effect of that shift on identity development in biracial and bicultural children and tensions between the communities of color.

Ms. Weston has a masters in Special Education from the University of Northern Colorado and a masters in Social Work from the University of Denver. She teaches multiculturalism and women's studies at the university level including classes in women's and Africana studies at the University of Northern Colorado, gender and communication and public speaking at Metropolitan State College, and sociology at the Community College of Denver. Ms. Weston has also been the Special Assistant to the President for Diversity Affairs for Naropa University and the state wide Community/Regional Coordinator, CWT Preventing HIB/AIDS for the Colorado Depart. of Public Health and Environment.

Ms. Weston has published numerous articles including "Multicultural Musings"—essays on multicultural/social justice issues, Naropa University website and newsletter, Boulder, Colorado; "Black Hair and Identity Politics," Urban Spectrum newspaper, Denver, Colorado; "Black Folks I Know and Other Commentary"—unpublished manuscript on biracial/bicultural issues; "Multiculturalism in the U.S."—an edited sourcebook for university use.

The avocations of fiber arts and handbuilding clay masks round out the list of her endeavors.

The Phoenix Rising

Sherryl N. Weston, M.A., M.S.W.

The Professional Path

I came to social work through the back door.

At the same time that my spirituality was coalescing, my interest in feminism, and in particular domestic violence and women's health, led me to volunteer work that gave me the first exposure to social work as a profession. I was trained as a volunteer at a domestic violence shelter where I found myself fascinated with the issues that brought women to that resource. I was also finding my career as a special education teacher exceedingly frustrating; I was always questioning the rules and regulations, challenging inequity, and concerning myself with the family problems that brought kids to the label of "emotionally disturbed." It was at that time I decided to change careers. I had heard that with a master's degree in any field one could get a job as a child protection caseworker. I took the necessary oral exam for my master's degree, and scored in the 90s. I began a social work career without the social work credential.

I did not listened to myself when I was in this, my first, master's program (special education). I began to see that I didn't want to be a special education teacher. I was attracted to people who were psychology majors. However, I was assured by others that teaching was a more secure job choice. (I believe these assurances were well intended but include a cultural bias about safety that I think comes from the black American history of a great respect for teaching.) I realize now that this dilemma was due to my status as a first generation college student. No one in my family had graduated from college before me, so I didn't have the professional mentoring that others get. I didn't have any idea what social work was, and my view of psychology was a vague image of a psychiatrist-like person sitting behind a desk. I stuck with what I thought I understood better. Once I was doing social work, several years went by before I learned that the profession had two branches: the macro or indirect and the clinical focus that became dominant as the "professionalization" of social work abandoned its community organizing and activist roots.

It was a child protection case involving the bride-price customs of the Hmong culture that thrust me into the cultural competence field. I was assigned the first Hmong case in my county and had to wade my way through the learning process about that culture and the way that the U.S. police and social services system clashed with their ways of viewing rape and marriage. I began the personal growth that would force me to assess my natural inclination toward intercultural issues as a professional asset. After developing a training program to teach the protocol I developed, a supervisor told me I should "take it on the road." There began my career as a cultural competence professional. I knew it was my calling. I began this career in the early 1990s, before so many others marketed themselves in this way.

I saw this profession as a sideline while at the same time keeping full time jobs that sucked me dry. I finally crashed and burned. I really thought there was something wrong with me.

I had been getting into hot water over what I now understand was a result of being liberal-leaning in very conventional environments. I was always one of very few who saw other ways of doing things, who rejected alliances to the status quo. In many instances, I have been exonerated for my ideas after my exit. It took awhile before I recognized that my values and who I was as an individual required a different setting to be successful. I also found that the very "professionalization" of social work was keeping me out of jobs that I could do with my eyes shut. I was forced to obtain a second masters, a Masters in Social Work (M.S.W.) although I had a master's degree in special education already. There was no program in my state that offered a Ph.D. in social work that would allow for my ten-plus years of successful skill-building and experience.

I found my M.S.W. program about 50 percent a waste of my time. Most of my classmates were 20 years my junior. I also found that many of us with years of experience were far more culturally competent than the curriculum in the program supported. Rarely was any student forced to truly examine his or her class, race, and heterosexual biases toward potential clients. Therefore, there are graduates of my program (so I have heard from colleagues) who are perpetuating their biases in their respective workplaces.

The Perfect Opportunity

I was lucky to come across the right job while I was still in school working on my M.S.W., my second masters. I knew by then that I wanted to help train therapists and teachers to be culturally competent. For many reasons, I thought that I had found the perfect place to begin doing just that. By then, I was a firm Unitarian Universalist which satisfied my search for a spiritual path that incorporated both activism and faith in action without the provincialism and cultural arrogance of others that I had encountered.

My perfect opportunity, as far as I could see, consited of three major elements. First, it was at a small, liberal, private university whose founder anchored its roots in the core belief that there is universal wisdom in all of the world's spiritual traditions.

My spirituality would fit in here! I could even call it my ministry and that concept would be understood.

Second, there was a desire on the part of certain segments of the leadership at this university to walk the talk and to respond to the growing awareness of the university's inability to recruit and retain students, staff, and faculty of color.

And third, a board member was generous and dug into her own pocket to fund the beginning of what would become the university's Office of Diversity Affairs.

Sound like the equation with rousing success after the equal sign? Not quite. Sound like an easy place to get the work done? Not really.

Studying the effects of internalized oppression, interlocking oppressions, world wisdom traditions, and cultural appropriation were key concepts in this work. My understanding of how they were relevant was also the place where the struggles began. For a large part, most people in that institution did not know what these concepts were. Even once my definitions were clarified, they were not immediately accepted or understood by everyone.

My Roots and How They Prepared Me for the Job

In my work as a consultant and trainer in cultural competence, I have drawn heavily on my experience as a baby boomer who grew up in an apolitical, widely traveled military family and who has continually had interaction with a variety of cultures, races, and sexual orientations. At times this has put me at odds with the party line of what should have been my main point of reference—U.S.-born blacks—for that is who I am, a North American-born black woman of African descent, though, like many of us, I also have both American Indian and European ancestors to point to.

In both all-black (American) gatherings with other social work colleagues and in all-white gatherings in my extended family of origin, I have often found myself a bit of an odd duck. When I had a British accent as a child; when I helped an immigrant negotiate our crazy legal systems; when I am the straight ally to the GLBTQI communities; when I am the only person in an all-Latino crowd who speaks Spanish; when I am the only black person present whose spiritual orientation is not exclusively Christian, I have had to develop a way to be in the world that kept me sane and, and at the same time, kept the critics at bay. I knew the work wouldn't be a piece of cake. I also knew that it is a rare person who holds as many kinds of close community connections as I do. In my professional settings, I have been praised for the ability to be a bridge and to speak to and from many different perspectives. I really did think that my ease in all these diverse worlds would make my job relatively easy to do. I was wrong!

The Job and the Resistance

In the beginning, my job as Special Assistant to the President for Diversity Affairs, was defined in extremely general terms. For supervision, it was attached to Academic Affairs instead of to the Office of the President. (The title of the position indicated attachment to the president.) I applied, got the job, and set about learning the issues at hand. Several immediate obstacles presented themselves: there had not been such a position before, so there was not office space or even a computer immediately available, and there was no solid plan in place. There was no independent administrative power attached to the position. There was a committee that had been meeting on a regular basis for some time, but even the committee had no administrative power or budget of its own. There was a crisis to be resolved concerning issues of cultural appropriation with African dance. There was also an ongoing conflict involving cultural appropriation that had been festering with the American Indian community.

There was a widely-held point of view, which some attributed (in error) to the religious teachings of the institution, that conflict and the expression of anger were weaknesses which should be handled by the individual through more intensive self-scrutiny and deeper spiritual practice. The result was an institutional reticence to address what some saw as individual, personal problems, equal to anyone else's pain or problem.

One of the stickier problems to be handled was that the demographic of the town where the institution is located is wealthy and 97 percent white. The part of the student body that was not white was made up of international students who had not been made aware of how racism issues may be relative to their experiences in the states and U.S. students who were transracially adopted or otherwise raised in situations that made them more comfortable with whites than with people of color. Some of the anger and resistance to challenging institutional oppression came from people of color for whom the concept of internalized oppression was foreign and/or scary. In the first year of my job, two Latino students left, citing my work as the reason. Meanwhile, students, staff, and faculty who were well-rooted in their cultures usually did not stay long, although most of them stopped by on their way out to tell me what I was doing was needed, but was not changing things fast enough to make it worth their stay.

Too many people at this institution thought the whole diversity discussion was irrelevant and that cultural appropriation was just "politically correct gatekeeping," preventing everyone's right to study or participate in whatever interested them in whatever fashion they felt comfortable. It did not matter that Hindus or blacks or Asians might feel marginalized, objectified, or offended.

The most difficult issue facing the institution was that there was not agreement on the definition of the core problem of how to deal with the "hierarchy of oppression"—the struggling among targeted groups and the outside influence that enables that struggle; of what racism is; of what contemporary language is appropriate to be using for describing the challenges at hand; and a deep, abiding resistance to the concept of making anything mandatory. The desire was to create an environment that would encourage each individual to choose to get on board with the diversity agenda.

On top of all of this was a budgetary situation that did not even sustain everything else that was needed. They certainly did not have the money to support me, my office, low-income students' needs, or pay for faculty-wide curriculum development resources. But mysteriously, the money did appear when it was needed to construct a new building elsewhere and to purchase new property which required expensive remodeling.

How the Work Got Done

I learned to identify allies on campus—real allies, the kind who were willing to take on the work that was hard for me to do because of the color of my skin and the assumptions that were made as a result. My upbringing played a huge role here, in my success in identifying the allies, but also in the extent to which I infuriated some. After awhile, I realized that the combination of a belief in my absolute equality to any white person and a refusal to play the coping mechanisms we are taught about getting along with white people meant that any white person who could be a colleague or good friend of mine had to be someone who could hear WHATEVER I had to say about race, class, and gender, just as any person of color in my life would. They had to already have significant, intimate, healthy relationships with people of color. They had to speak up about things they did not have to speak up about. They had to have ongoing activities that put them in the ally position on a regular basis. And I found those people at this institution.

I found them by seeing how they walked the talk. I believe that this type of institution attracted certain kinds of people, many of whom were outside of mainstream white society. A portion of these people had been lifelong advocates in the meaningful ways. The ones who could be my allies stuck out almost immediately. I had learned, through my other "bad" work experiences, how to see through superficial overtures. As far as I know, I was never wrong. A few have become real friends, as good as any I have had in my life. Because of the nature of this place, I am not sure it would be as easy in other settings. People at this institution wore their real selves on their sleeve a little more often than in places that are more conventional.

Another skill that worked was having learned to be creative, not always looking at conventional wisdom. I had to know when to say what and how to say it, but never, ever compromising the truth. I had to use what I knew about the inside of certain mindsets to work around or with them as necessary. I had to trust my instincts and recognize that most of the time there would be key people who would not understand what was necessary but would work around that by empowering entities or individuals with the information they needed to have a step up. Being someone who knew a lot about the populations outside the ones to which I belong came in handy on more than one occasion.

I had to remember to play hard outside of work and set strong boundaries around my personal needs. I had to develop an even thicker skin than the one I already had. I learned too well what the limits to my patience were, and after about four years, I knew it was time to stop. It was important to stop while I still had control of me and my limits. Very early in the job, it became clear that it was far more work than one person could do, and I never allowed the expectations to exceed the reasonable.

What Got Done?

The beginnings of many infrastructure elements had been forged. Definitions of the problems were firmly formulated, although the resistance was not totally squelched. Terms like "internalized oppression" and what that meant for the kind of student of color who came to the school were better understood. The resignation of the president resulted in a search committee that, at least, had a version of cultural competence at its center. A multicultural student center was started. A version of the document that I and two others wrote became the institution's cultural appropriation policy and was finalized within months of my departure. And, I had the most awesome going away reception that anyone could ever imagine. You could have filled a bucket with the tears. (And not just mine.)

I believe that the work went as far as it did because we had the acceptance of the mind, body, and spirit connection, which forces people out of their heads, at least some. The other reason that cannot be dismissed is that there now are more white allies than ever, and some of them are looking for what to do next. Many of these people are attracted to the institution where I worked. Many more exist in other places. One of my main recommendations to white allies is that their work is more to work on other white people (and with straight allies on the queer community, and so on) than it is to "help the downtrodden." There are no more excuses for having their feet stuck in the denial cement.

I had risen from the ashes. The phoenix in me rose! I usually was able not to take things personally, even if someone tried to make it personal. I learned to accept that this diversity and equity onion that we are peeling takes a long time to chop. I know that ringing ears and runny noses and bloodied fingers abound. Knowing that I sharpened the blade is good enough for now. My calling remains, but it is active in other places and in other ways.

Nancy J. Nelson

Dr. Nancy J. Nelson is the Director of the African American Education Program at Eastern Washington University. She earned her Ph.D. in Education at Walden University. She has a master of arts in Education and a bachelor of arts degree in Liberal Arts from Antioch University, Seattle. Her studies emphasized African-American issues, history, and history in music.

Dr. Nelson has spoken and performed on African-American topics at several venues including Notre Dame University, Eastern Washington University, North Idaho College, Centralia Community College, Spokane Falls Community College, Airway Heights Correctional Center, local elementary and high schools as well as the Washington State Historical Museum. Additionally, she is a vocalist, poet, and doll artist.

As a vocalist, Dr. Nelson performs educational programs on the history of Negro spirituals and on issues involving African-American history and culture, domestic violence, and youth. The dolls she creates, which have been displayed in museums, libraries, and on university campuses, reflect events and time periods in African-American history.

African-American Studies Majors

Nancy J. Nelson, Ph.D.

African Americans who major in African-American studies are subjected to countless accounts of suffering, murder, rape, torture, molestation, lynching, and other acts of violence committed against African Americans. Emotional responses may include feelings of hopelessness, depression, and thoughts of suicide. Added to the problem is the lack of understanding from students, administrators and faculty on some campuses. Faculty and other students do not realize the emotional stress that acts of racism and learning a difficult history can have on African American students. The question is raised; can majoring in African-American studies increase the suicide rate of African Americans?

According to Poussaint and Alexander (2000), stress related illness and self-destructive behaviors of African Americans are due to racism from the legacy of slavery. After "a confrontation or perceived victimization" (p. 22) the chance of suicide increases.

Social problems, particularly those that seem to be unsolvable, such as poverty and unemployment, can lead to a sense of hopelessness and depression. Urban youth who know a murder victim are two times more likely to commit suicide than the populace as a whole, while those who witness a stabbing are three times more likely (Joe and Kaplan, 2001). A suicide attempt leads to a greater risk for subsequent attempts (Lyon, Benoit, O'Donnell and Getson, 2000).

Suicide among African Americans, particularly for males, has rapidly increased during the period following the civil rights movement, which allowed for greater integration. In addition, black studies programs began at several universities, giving the false impression of acceptance of African Americans and the legitimizing of African American history. In 1970, the suicide rate for African-American males was 7.9 per 100,000, while in 1997 the rate had increased to 10.9 per 100,000 (Poussaint and Alexander, 2000). While the study of African-American history and issues can be empowering, for some it is destructive.

As the director of African-American education at a predominantly white state university, in an area that is notorious for white supremast and neonazi groups, I must process feelings of oppression daily. Studying African-American history and keeping up to date on race issues can take a toll. Added to this, I must support African-American students as they process their history and deal with racist issues on and off campus. African-American students speak with clinched throats and with agonizing pain in their eyes as they learn our past and battle the racism. After a class that discussed the lynching of African Americans, one student was unable to look away from the swinging cord on a screen. When the Young Republicans hosted an Affirmative Action bake sale, the African-American students expressed such pain that my heart cried a mother's grief, again, as I had the day before and the day before that. Another student realized that the reason she was struggling with an assignment in African-American history was because she was being depressed by the subject.

What decides which direction an African American majoring in African-American studies will chose? Will it be the road to suicide as with a predominant Spokane civil rights attorney and a 34-year-old university professor? Is there a way to insure a positive direction? We need to recognize, study, and understand the possible effects of studying African-American history and develop support needed for positive response.

The purpose of the following letter is to broaden the awareness of the possible problems of studying and majoring in African-American studies, particularly at predominantly white universities, so that preventive measures may be put into place. The letter also explains some of the suffering of one who works with issues of race and supporting students on predominantly white campus.

To you who have discovered the shell that I leave behind, plain brown and now still, and to the few with tears to shed and to the ones who ask why, I leave this explanation. I wish it were simpler for you and apologize for its length. If I was simply having problems or if my heart were broken from a fallen love, you could say, "Ah, poor thing. Why didn't she get some help?" and then return to your lives.

But my story is long and deep. Many times I have asked, cried, begged for your help. Perhaps you did not know how to help or perhaps you did not hear. I think more that you did not understand the depth of my pain or the exhaustion of my struggle. After reading these pages you still may not understand. Even now that causes me to cry out in agony.

It wasn't you alone who shut your eyes. Nor do I blame any of you for failing to save me from taking my life. I have journeyed through this pain long enough to know that you do not recognize it and may not still. But you at least deserve an explanation for the coldness of this form that has hopefully been found with eyes closed so that no one must look into their faded darkness.

I have chosen not to be politically correct as I have had to live. As I will not be here to hear the judgment that is placed upon me, I do not care. It is this caring that has helped to bring me to this place, or to this time would perhaps be more accurate. By now you may not even be caring of the language that I use as long as I get to the reason so that you will be able to complete the paperwork, close the chapter and go on with your lives.

Even with my skin now an ashen tone it is obvious that I am or was a woman of color, an African American, a black woman, a sista!, a girlfriend!, a Negro, a Negress, a descendant of slaves, former slaves, and from rich African kingdoms. Less obvious is my being a descendant from people without color, Caucasians, European Americans, whites, slave owners, enslavers, brutal people from Europe who I have never known and who have displayed no interest in knowing me. I dutifully learned their collective histories during the many years that I was forced to receive what was said to be a well-rounded, accurate education of history. So I feel that I have given them enough of my time, mind, and energy, enough of my life.

As I think about it, it is due to this side of my ancestry that I have taken my life. How can I blame you in your innocence, you who I have never met, when it was my hand that accomplished this deed? There is really no one else to blame. I am now, I pray, at peace; a peace I have never known in life.

Now you may be demanding of me an explanation, direct and honest, since you now feel accused and responsible. You are weary of the tales of how black skinned people suffer, do without, are treated as unequals and on and on. Yet have you ever thought of what I have lived because of your racism, your ideas, the treatment I have had to endure from you? I cannot wholly blame you, not personally, because I do not even know you. And you are, of course, not responsible for the choices I have made nor the direction my life has taken.

You did not force me to dig so deeply into history that I covered my ears, screaming the suffering of millions of ancestors who wanted to be heard, who wanted everyone to know that even in death they could not find rest. Rest can only come when their stories have been heard. They rushed at me to tell them but it was too much for me, so much all at once that I cried out with them. I ran leaving them still in their disturbed darkness.

Though it was not my will, I had to go back. It was my destiny to hear them, to help them, to attempt to free them. But they had to slow down. They had to talk to me one at a time of lost sons and daughters, of longing to find fathers and mothers, of rapes and sales and laboring hard in the fields. They could not just tell of their lashings but held me down so I would feel each blow while staring into the twisted face of the one doing the deed. My back bled. My voice was gone from ignored screams. My eyes were drained of tears. I, as they had, eventually stopped begging for mercy for there was none in the eyes of the one who unleashed his fury on my back after having risen from laying between my legs.

So they sat with me on a small patch of grass in the shadow of a tree. The sparkling cool river ran at our feet. I could see others waiting their turns in the distance, fearful that they may again frighten me off before their stories were told. They spoke looking down or off into the distance, as if I would not believe the horror that was their lives and that the peace they were promised in death did not come. They felt, truly believing that

I could carry their stories; that I would tell them to those still alive. Then maybe they would find rest. Some reached out their cold hands from tattered dress and shirt sleeves to touch me for emphasis or to be sure that I was of the living. When they were done, they would gracefully rise as if a burden had indeed been lifted. They would leave only to have another quickly take their place.

One stayed longer than the others. Her dark face had a familiarness. "Great-grandmother?" I whispered in my heart. From her the story was the hardest, my flesh and my blood, the one responsible for my existence. For her I had my own questions, knowledge I needed. I explained to her that I did not want this calling—that it was too hard—too painful to carry so many voices and so many hundreds of years. Finally she stilled me with a gentle touch of her hand. I laid my head in her lap as she stroked my hair, promising to give me what strength she could. Her shining black face had known no smiles. She could not save me as she could not save herself or the children she bore her master.

So now you see me as insane, claiming to have talked with the spirits of those long dead. Perhaps it was a dream or only a description of how one may feel majoring in this study of Black lives in this rich country. Let me put it in more acceptable terms for you so you will understand how one is "called." Fight if they will, they must eventually follow the path that has been laid for them; fighting and kicking as I have done, in the end there is no resistance.

We continue the struggle for rights to a full life in the United States. There is no top to this mountain that we must climb, only continuous rough terrain with always the possibility of falling. There are those who believe that we should forget our past, our history, our ancestors, who we are, where we are from, our experiences and our accomplishments. I was told by supporters that if I helped one, changed one mind or got one person to a least think, then I was successful. Yet it was those who I could not reach, whose eyes burned into mine with distain, who remained deep in my memory. You have not had to live as I have lived. You have not had to think, as I have had to think. You can shop without being followed. In airports your bags are not dusted for signs of gunpowder even though you have never in your life touched a gun. You do not know the complete list of what are considered to be weapons when questioned at the Canadian border. Your food has never been spat in before being served to you in restaurants. You are waited on in stores, never skipped over or ignored as if you are invisible. You don't have to think that at times being invisible would make your life simpler.

I studied. I read. I listened and I watched. I took in the history, trying to numb the feelings but being thrown into the dark pit of tar. It is the fate of an artist to go too far to understand. I have tried to accomplish my calling to the best of my ability, but it has proven to be too much for me. As my words rolled off deaf ears I have tried not to let the stern faces and folded arms affect my mission; though at times, I was haunted by those piercing blue eyes. The hardest to bear was the fear in the eyes of the blond haired children as my brown body merely walked past. The continuous frustration of not being heard, believed, understood or taken seriously has taken its toll. The miles I have traveled to go so short a distance only to lose much more has taken its toll.

I should stop now, but you—you must always know why, have it totally explained so you don't have to think, so I am forced to continue with this intense pain. Give me a moment to close my eyes and calm some of my spirit so I can go on.

After a news event of the murder of a black man while in jail or in prison or at a traffic stop or the mistreatment of a black child or yet another unsolved rape of a black woman or child, or if I am denied yet another service, talked down to, or have my success labeled as "Well, I guess they have to fill their quotas," I began to look for a place in the world that I can live safe and free. My mind scans the world's countries to find one that is not tainted with prejudice and fear of my dark skin, golden brown, shiny and soft.

There was a call, or another call, of another hate incident at another university and I reach for a bottle of pills that I don't have or didn't have until now. I have been saving them to have just enough or maybe one or two extra. There is no room for failure in this ending for I am too tired to try again. It seems that with this constant work of equality and equal rights that we are still taking unsteady baby steps, one forward and two back. We are always looking up the steep jagged mountain—never seeing the last peak. There is no end to this work. There is no time to lay down the weapons of war. There is only falling back into the trenches while bullets fly over head, taking a breath, two breaths with eyes closed and chest beating. Then we reload and jump back into the line of fire.

Have I explained a reason to help you to understand? I have noticed during my short life that people insist on having everything explained to them quickly and shortly. They do not want to have to look anything up or feel any guilt, sorrow or pain. I do not offer any apologies as I have had to for my entire life as I am tired, just tired. It is because of you that I have over compensated, over-tipped because you believed that I wouldn't tip you. Tired from over smiling muscles so you wouldn't fear me; from being overly honest making sure that you saw I could be trusted as you glanced out of the corner of your eye, as you never tired of following me through stores; as you crossed streets and danced away from me in your speech because you feared the darkness of my skin interpreted as darkness in me.

When our enslaved ancestors were so down trodden that no word or touch could help the, they would let it be known through the singing in a slow moan, "Sometimes I feel like a mother-less child, a long way from home, a long way from home." I cannot count the many times I moaned so low.

My death will be quick and sweet as the suffering I have lived with has been too much to add to. All I long for is relief. Do not cry for my death but shed tears for my life. I will wander through a dense darkness to the river that so many have crossed over. I will take hold of the thin rough black hand reaching out for mine, younger and light brown. She will say to me "It's alright, Baby, great-grandmother understands," and I will be at peace.

References

Joe, S. and Kaplan, M.S. "Suicide among African American Men," *Suicide and Life-Threatening Behavior* (31), 2000, 106-121.

Lyon, M.E., Benoit, M., O'Donnell, R.M., and Getson, P.R. "Assessing African American Adolescents' Risk for Suicide Attempts: Attachment Theory." *Adolescence* (35), 2000, 137, 121-134.

Poussaint, A.F. and Alexander, A. *Lay My Burden Down: Unraveling Suicide and the Mental Health Crisis Among African-Americans.* (Boston, MA: Beacon Press, 2000).

Roland B. Smith, Jr.

Dr. Roland B. Smith, Jr., is Associate Provost and Adjunct Professor of Education and Sociology at Rice University. He has mentored many Mellon Mays Undergraduate Fellows and others to pursue their Ph.D. He teaches ethnographic research methods and chairs the Rice University's Educational Outreach Council. Dr. Smith came to Rice after 23 years at the University of Notre Dame, where he served as Executive Assistant to the President, concurrent associate professor of sociology, founding Director of the Center for Educational Opportunity—including Upward Bound, Educational Talent Search, and McNair. Before working in higher education, Dr. Smith was a research intern in the United States Senate and manpower planner for the city of South Bend, Indiana.

Dr. Smith served as Chair of the National Association of Presidential Assistants in Higher Education and member of the Martin Luther King, Jr., Federal Holiday Commission. More recently, he served as chair of the Black Caucus of the American Association for Higher Education and member of the Board of Directors for the American Conference of Academic Deans and the Bowie State University Board of Visitors. Currently, he serves on the Board of Directors for the Harvard Alumni Association.

A native of Washington, DC, Dr. Smith holds a B.A. in Anthropology and Sociology from Bowie State University. He also holds a M.P.A. from Indiana University and an Ed.D. from Harvard University. He is married and has two children.

Muses of a Mentor: A Tribute to the Elders

Roland B. Smith, Jr., Ed.D.

July 1, 2003 marked my thirtieth year as a professional in higher education. I spent all of that time at predominantly white universities in a number of capacities. Since achieving that career milestone, I have been more reflective regarding my journey as an educator and all that it embodies for me—teacher, colleague, administrator, mentor, and facilitator of educational access and institutional change. The road has been complete with ups and downs and sudden twists and turns that no one could have predicted. For all practical purposes, it has been an extraordinary journey that began when I graduated from Bowie State College in 1969 with a major in anthropology-sociology and a minor in political science. Bowie, the oldest of the three historically black institutions in Maryland, was part of the old, segregated state college system.

My purpose in this reflection is to share and explore two life episodes that made my professional journey possible and, in the process, symbolically pay tribute to the many individuals who have touched my life, including Manpower Planning Director Isaiah Jackson of South Bend, Indiana; Dean Roselle Boyd of Indiana University; Harvard Professor Charles V. Willie; and Notre Dame President Rev. Edward A. Malloy, CSC, to name a few. I remain forever grateful to them all.

The first episode, which I call "Second Chance at an Early Age," occurred while I was in elementary school. The second episode, which I call "Accidental Protester," took place while I was in college. Both have played a major role in the formation and development of my outlook and interest in issues of access, opportunity, and mentoring at all levels of education. Above all, these episodes give a historical context to my passion for mentoring; that is the joy I get in contributing in some small way to students and young educators—young being defined here as those younger than me. In a real sense, these episodes represent my version of what Bennis and Thomas (2003) have labeled "crucibles," which are those defining or transforming moments in one's life.

Second Chance at an Early Age

Can you imagine the plight of an African-American boy who enters the sixth grade reading on a third grade level? It certainly does not take much imagination to envision a dead ended life for such a boy. Teachers, parents, and others could easily envision the boy as having almost no potential for educational success (Scheffler, 1985). I was that boy in 1957 in Washington, DC, a city that was still struggling with the Supreme Court's decision in Brown v. Board of Education. Mrs. Howard, also African American, was my teacher. Before that year, Mrs. Howard knew me only as one of the kids in the northeast neighborhood of Brookland. She was known among the kids as someone to be feared. Some described her as "mean." Needless to say, I was not looking forward to her class. I wondered why kids called her "Eagle Eyes" until I witnessed her in action. She would write on the blackboard and simultaneously call out a student by name for whispering to his or her neighbor or being otherwise distracting to the class.

It did not take me long to understand how to be on her good side and otherwise escape her wrath. I tried to be strategic in my participation in class discussions on current topics, relying on conversations I heard around the dinner table and on our 13-inch console television at home. I absolutely hated to read aloud. I remember it as being among my most humiliating educational experiences and would try my best to become invisible during reading time. When called upon, my heart would race. I would break into a cold sweat as I stumbled haltingly through a passage transposing or skipping words. Much of that year was a blur, but I clearly remember the series of events that Mrs. Howard orchestrated and, in the process, revealed to me what a caring person she was. First, she arranged to have my eyes tested, which revealed something she already suspected. I needed glasses. Second, she arranged a conference with my parents and me and revealed not only that I needed glasses but that I had a learning disorder. Following the parent conference, my grandparents helped to pay for my first pair of glasses, and my parents gave Mrs. Howard permission to place me in an after-school reading program and a reading clinic on Saturdays. Mrs. Howard's third, and at the time most painful, step was to arrange for me to attend summer school and then repeat the sixth grade. In doing this, Mrs. Howard gave me a second chance. But she did much, much more. She dramatically increased my potential for future academic success and set in motion events that have helped me to touch many lives.

Accidental Protester

It was August of 1967. I was excited about returning to Bowie State College to start my junior year. After all, I had made the Dean's List as a sophomore after struggling through my freshman year. I had been elected vice president of the Student Government Association (SGA), serving as chair of its legislative branch. I had completed my second summer of working full time at the Washington Hospital Center in the central supply unit as an orthopedic attendant and had switched to working there only on the weekends—two 12-hour shifts. This arrangement had a distinct advantage. I was able to concentrate on my studies and campus activities during the week without the distraction of work.

These achievements were all very important to me because I almost did not go to college and almost had to leave once I got there. I emerged from my freshmen year only to learn that the money my parents had saved for my college education was enough only to cover my freshman year. I had my parents' love and unwavering support, but I had to find a way to support my college education.

In any event, I was ready for a busy and productive junior year in student government and in my courses. I looked forward to concentrating on courses in my major, anthropology-sociology.

We had a new president, Dr. Samuel L. Myers, Sr., having succeeded Dr. Henry, who had served for 25 years. With a Harvard Ph.D. in economics, Dr. Myers had been a professor and dean at Morgan State College, and he came to Bowie State College after a stint at the U.S. State Department. His very formal and highly intellectual demeanor was accentuated by an array of bow ties he wore—a different one for every occasion.

The SGA president and I wasted no time in getting things organized. He, as SGA president, headed up the executive branch, which included the class presidents. I, as vice president, headed up the legislative branch, which included the presidents of all official student organizations. It did not take long for things to heat up on campus.

Suddenly and without warning, the SGA president resigned, and I was installed as president to finish out the year. Students, many of whom would quietly lament the poor conditions of the physical plant, began to complain openly about a range of shortcomings. One rumor claimed that Bowie's presidents had routinely returned unspent funds to the state each year. Although he was only months into his presidency, many of us began to direct our displeasure at Dr. Myers. However, the semester ended without incident.

Things began to heat up again at the start of the spring semester. First, while enrolled in an intersession course, I was one of several students who learned that Governor Spiro Agnew had partially funded the college's capital budget, thus preventing physical plant improvements, including a new building approved by the board of trustees. Second, word spread that a popular faculty member did not get tenure. Third, one of the women's dorms experienced repeated power failures.

Equipped with the new information about Governor Agnew's misleading budget appropriation, we began the process of redirecting our complaints from Dr. Myers to the board of trustees and finally to the governor. It was during this period that my relationship with Dr. Myers began to deepen. I did not fully appreciate it then, but Dr. Myers mentored me as we met in his office to debate the issues at hand. He helped me to understand that while our strategies differed, we had the same goal—improving Bowie.

After weeks of meetings, letters, and phone calls to restore funding and otherwise increase support for the college, we got no meaningful response from the governor. Most of the legislators we met were very supportive; however, state law prevented the legislature from increasing the governor's annual budget. Our request was simple at this juncture. We wanted a meeting with the governor. His only response was to send a fact-finding team in a failed attempt to pacify us. Dr. Myers later described a key visit of the team's leader as a "fiasco" (Witcover, 1997).

Our next course of action as students to get the governor's attention was to stage a one-day boycott of classes on March 27, 1968, and encourage students to go to the campus library, a very small building with limited holdings. Tensions continued to build when there was no further response from Governor Agnew. On the evening of Friday, March 29, we staged a largely symbolic campus takeover. Saturday morning the governor deployed 150 state troopers with riot gear to the campus, along with the state's attorney general, Francis Burch. While the students were occupying Banneker Hall, the administration/classroom building (which was always open for students to come and study), I was among those in the president's office along with Mr. Burch, Dr. Myers, and other officials. Mr. Burch was on the phone telling the governor we had broken no laws since we were entitled to use the building. He and Dr. Myers persuaded the governor to meet with us if we would return to what he called a "state of normalcy." In the heat of the moment, I witnessed Dr. Myers's calm demeanor with simultaneous feelings of anger, puzzlement, and respect.

We reluctantly agreed and vacated the building that afternoon on the strength of a promise of a meeting with the governor. On Monday, we returned to classes and waited for the promised phone call to schedule a meeting with the governor. By Wednesday, there was no call. Having concluded that the governor reneged on his promise, we drafted a list of grievances to deliver to him. That evening, we began planning a massive trip to the Maryland State House the following day to deliver the grievances and chartered two buses. By this time we had the full support and guidance of the local, state, and national levels of the NAACP. We established a dress and conduct code, requiring the men to wear dress shirts with ties and the women to wear skirts or dresses. Everyone was encouraged to bring books to read while we waited.

Bowie was the most integrated institution of higher education in Maryland with a 15 percent white student enrollment drawn from the nearby city of Bowie and from a new suburban community. In fact, a relative of a white student alerted us that Governor Agnew would be in his office the following day.

The next day around 1:00 p.m., a caravan of buses and cars carrying over 230 students and a few faculty members embarked on the short ride to Annapolis. We arrived at the State House about 1:30 p.m. Once inside, I, along with the five other members of the student leadership team, proceeded up the main stairway leading to the governor's office. The governor's aide, flanked by state troopers, intercepted us halfway up the stairs and firmly suggested that we leave because "the governor was not in and could not be reached." After declining his suggestion, we rejoined the rest of the students in the main hallway and sat along the walls so as not to block the entrances, and we intermittently sang civil rights songs.

At about 3:00 p.m., the aide came back down the stairs to report that Governor Agnew said he would have us arrested and close down the college indefinitely if we did not leave the building by 5:00 p.m. For the next two hours, we deliberated the pros and cons of backing down to Governor Agnew yet one more time. Minutes before the deadline, members of the student leadership team indicated that they would support my decision. Feeling that we had to take a stand, I decided to stay—so did 227 other students. A few minutes after 5:00 p.m., the building superintendent declared the building, which was also filled with media and spectators, closed. We students were the only people declared as trespassers. We agreed not to resist arrest or insight violence. I was the first student arrested. By 5:30 p.m., we were led off to waiting school buses and taken to the county jail. Once photographed and fingerprinted, we were placed in two riot cells—one for males, the other for females. The events of the preceding weeks had taken their toll, leaving me more exhausted than frightened. I fell asleep on one of the mattresses brought into the cell and thrown on the floor.

I was awakened suddenly by another student at about 7:15 p.m. He shouted, "Roland! Roland! They killed Martin Luther King!" At that moment a sense of rage and anger jerked its way through my body. I had never felt such rage. It scared me that for the first time in my life I wanted to hurt someone. As we sat helpless in that riot cell lamenting the sad state of affairs in America, I concluded that if we abandon the strategy of nonviolent social change, Dr. King would have died in vain. At that very moment, I made a commitment to myself to pursue nonviolent social and educational change wherever I found myself.

In the weeks and months after that April 4th, Dr. Myers continued to meet with me, each time sharing with me new insights into the culture and politics of higher education.

The Bowie episode forced me to confront the ugliness that still haunts America in a variety of forms. Dr. Myers, in his own way of mentoring, offered me a glimpse into the complicated, and often lonely, world of an African-American leader in higher education.

Creating Meaning from Crucible Experiences

Bennis and Thomas (2003) stress "the power of the crucible" in leaders young and old. Two points emerge from their study that offer particular relevance to this story. First, crucibles can come from experiences that are positive or negative, tragic or joyous. Second, the most important outcome emerges by "creating meaning out of the crucible experiences" with the ability to "integrate them into one's life."

For me, Mrs. Howard, Dr. Myers, and Dr. King are symbols for something much greater than any one person can be. They represent a commitment to future generations. From Mrs. Howard, I learned to look for potential in students where it may not be apparent and to take action that will increase their potential for success. From Dr. Myers and the Bowie experience, I learned the importance of teachable moments in the midst of chaos and conflict. I also learned the value of negotiating common ground. From Dr. King's life, I learned the role of commitment to the greater good. They all taught me the powerful lesson of reaching back to help those coming behind me.

I began integrating these and other lessons into my life in 1973 upon my transition from government service to higher education as the assistant director of an Upward Bound program, and later as its director. Eager to make a difference in the lives of the program's students, I was caught off guard—perhaps naively—by the many battle fronts I faced in mentoring minority high school students who were potential first-generation college graduates. The first front involved winning over the local school system's teachers, counselors, and administrators to identify students with promise. My notion of potential sometimes differed from theirs. The second front involved those at the university who did not understand why it should reach out to high school students who had little or no chance of entering its halls as undergraduates. The third front involved parents or guardians, many of whom felt a sense of ambivalence at the prospect of losing their child to the world of college. The fourth front involved the bureaucracy and politics of the federal government that appeared to work against the best interest of the students of the program. At the center were the students themselves, who sometimes worked against their own best interests—much the way I did at times in my interactions with the likes of Mrs. Howard and Dr. Myers. Almost instinctively taking pages from their books, I embarked on a professional journey to engage these fronts, which compelled me to incorporate the goal of mentoring others as I moved through what I have come to describe as "my nontraditional academic career matrix." My cultivation approach to mentoring has often been in conflict with the "weed out" culture that has been common among predominantly white universities. My goal in this regard has been to do my part in bridging the old "excellence versus equity" divide and, in the process, redefine both terms within the context of our ever-changing world. As it turns out, helping my students and young professionals find safe spaces to learn and grow has also fortified me professionally and personally. As Ramsden (1998) suggests, "enabling others" is one of the "responsibilities of university leadership." My experiences suggest that enabling others is also a benefit of leadership in the academy.

Whatever small contributions attributed to me by those whose lives I have touched are the contributions of countless ancestors who survived crucibles far more horrific, or exhilarating, than any of us today can imagine. Recounting my crucibles reminds me that our charge as mentors is to accept proudly the baton from our ancestors, do our part with honor as long as we are able, and pass the baton confidently to the next generation of educational leaders and mentors.

References

Bennis, W.G., and Thomas, R.J., *Geeks & Geezers: How Era, Values, and Defining Moments Shape Leaders* (Boston: Harvard Business School Press, 2002).

Ramsden, P., *Learning to Lead in Higher Education* (New York: Routledge, 1998).

Scheffler, I., *Of Human Potential: An Essay in the Philosophy of Education* (Boston: Routledge and Kegan Paul, 1985).

Witcover, J., *The Year the Dream Died: Revisiting 1968 in America* (New York: Warner Books, 1997).

Part 2

Stories from Graduate School, My Gender and My Race

Diary of a Superwoman   LaTashia R. Reedus

From Disappointment to Purpose   Terri M. Hurdle

On the Road to Success   Ryan J. Davis

Just Do It—I Did It   Juliana M. Mosley-Anderson

LaTashia R. Reedus

LaTashia R. Reedus currently serves as the Director of Multicultural Student Affairs at Mount Union College in Alliance, Ohio. A native of Cincinnati, Ohio and graduate of Walnut Hills High School, she received her B.A. in dual majors of African-American Studies and Sociology from the University of Cincinnati in 1993. She received her M.A. in Sociology from Ohio State University in 1996, where she also worked as a graduate teaching assistant and a graduate research assistant. Her academic focus centers on issues of race/ethnicity and higher education.

In her current position, Ms. Reedus is responsible for the daily operations of the Multicultural Student Affairs office whose primary function is to serve as a resource for students of color in matters of academic, social, cultural, and personal well-being. During her tenure at Mount Union College, she has also served as an academic advisor and course instructor in classes that focus on issues of race and race relations. She also teaches in the Department of African-American Studies and serves as the advisor to the Black Student Union and the Black Cultural Center at Mount Union College.

Mrs. Reedus' professional activities include the Ohio College Personnel Association and the John D. O'Bryant National Think Tank (JDOTT) where she serves as the Vice President of Finance/Secretary. She is involved in Girl Scouts of America, Inner-City League soccer coach, and is a member of The House of the Lord Church (Akron, Ohio) and Alpha Kappa Alpha Sorority, Inc.

Mrs. Reedus resides in Akron, Ohio with her husband, Derrick, and their three children, Derrick, Jr., BrieAnna, and Sienna.

Diary of a Superwoman
LaTashia R. Reedus, M.A.

A Day in the Life...

"Where did you come from, and why are you not asleep?" I find myself asking this question of my 14-month-old daughter as I sit at the computer to work on my submission for the second volume of Our Stories. Derrick, Jr., and BrieAnna went to bed 30 minutes ago, but Sienna refuses to go down without a fight. Inevitably, I have to stop what I am doing to take her to the other room so that I can get some work done while my eyes are still halfway open. Even from the computer, I can hear her crying, not too happy to be sitting with daddy but realizing that she has no choice at the moment. For a moment, I think about getting up to get her and putting her to sleep, but I realize that if I do that, I am just as likely to drift off as she is. And of course, that would put me behind—

even further—in all of the things that I have to do before tomorrow begins. Such is the world of the Professional Black Woman/Mother/Wife/ Student, also known as "Superwoman." When some asks me (and others in my situation) "How do you do it," I often want to respond, "that's a good question—can I pencil you in for a response three weeks from tomorrow?!?!?"

Wife. Mother. Professional. Sister/girlfriend. Christian. Black. Female. All of these things are an integral part of who I am and why I am that very person. I love my role as a wife and mother of three. My family makes it all worth while. I love my kids, and my husband is my soulmate; I would be incomplete without him. As a professional working in the area of multicultural student affairs, I realize that this is my calling. All of the students that I serve are also my children, except without the labor pains. My sisters and girlfriends keep me sane, allowing me to be just one of the girls as we share our lives together. My faith and relationship with God brings me through each day with its highs and lows and keeps me grounded in what is important. As a black person in America, I love my people and see us as resilient, ever pressing on in the midst of it all. And as a woman, I realize that I am responsible for nurturing all who depend on me, no matter who they are. But as much as I love these roles, they all demand so much of my time and energy that I wonder, "How can I continue at this pace and still maintain my sanity?"

My Journey to Superwoman Begins...

I graduated from the University of Cincinnati (UC) in 1993 with a double major in sociology and African-American studies. Like many students, it took me a minute to figure out that this is what I was meant to do. I came to UC intent on majoring in biology and eventually pursuing a Ph.D. with the hopes of doing research. Unfortunately, at the time, chemistry had other plans for me, so I changed to undecided and concentrated on general education requirements. Eventually I fell in love with a class in African-American studies as well as sociology, and I decided to combine the best of both worlds. I have always had a fascination with the social interaction between individuals and society, especially as it pertains to "black folk." I decided to pursue a graduate degree in sociology with the goal of becoming a professor at a large institution. Little did I know that the future, or shall I say God, had other ideas for me.

The early part of my first year as a graduate student at Ohio State University was one of the worst times of my life. I saw the other side of higher education with its ugly politics, and what I felt was a department that did not always live up to its rhetoric. For those of us, both black and white, who desired to have work and family, or who came with a family, there was often not much support. The focus seemed to be more on research and journals, teaching classes, thesis and dissertations, and the whole sordid politics of academia. There did not appear to be the needed focus on helping students achieve and maintain a balance between personal and professional life, unless you found it from individual faculty members. Couple that with the fact that there were not a lot of faces that looked like me, and it was a virtual breeding ground for discontent among many of the black students, especially the black female students. There were two black faculty members in the Sociology department at that time (one male, one female), and I gravitated towards both of them. Surprisingly, I became closer to the male professor, Dr. Clyde Franklin. Not only was he a source of support and refuge for me, but he helped me stay focused on why I was there and how to stay true to myself and the goals that I had set.

In retrospect, I believe that the reasons why I became so close to Dr. Franklin are more apparent now than they were at the time. Dr. Franklin was one of a small contingent of people who really taught me how to play the game when it came to education and dealing with "white folk" at the level of higher education. But he was only the second person that I had known—as a mentor—who had shown me that I could have my career goals and my family goals, as well as a few other things. It didn't have to be an either-or situation or a "career first, family second" mentality. Truth be told, the other person who taught me how to play the game was also a black man. As I reflect, I realize that I did not have a black female as a professional role model until well after I had figured out—or so I thought—how to have it all.

When I think back on the female professors I had in college, I note that they were overwhelmingly white. And let's face it, there just was not a lot that I had in common with any of these white women. Even now I can count on one hand the number of white females that I consider more than just an acquaintance or colleague. I had even fewer black female professors, but while we could relate on issues of race and the politics of being a black woman, none of them had the same family situation that I desired to have. As the oldest of five children—all females—I always knew that I wanted a family. At the time, family to me meant (1) a professional husband and (2) no less than three, but no more than five children. Simple and to the point. None of that 2.5 kids that we used to hear so much about. However, the female faculty and administrators that I saw often had only one child. Two kids? That was pushing it for most of these women. Or, they often started their family at a much later age than when I had intended, usually somewhere between the ages of 32 and 35. Many had "significant others," but few had spouses.

Did I mention that I was already engaged when I arrived at Ohio State? My husband and I had been dating for a little over two years when I left for graduate school. Derrick was finishing his senior year at UC when I started the first year of my master's program. My mentor and director of Ethnic Programs and Services at UC—Dr. P. Eric Abercrumbie—used to call Derrick my "stalker". We knew early that what we had was "the real thing." Although I hated to be separated, we knew it was only temporary. In fact, it was his support that got me through that first year, just as it gets me through my daily grind today. So you can imagine my irritation when a female faculty member suggested that I "put school and the master's degree first and marriage second." Even now I get angry when I think of how a female professor would say this to a female graduate student. What happened to the professional mentoring that is so crucial in helping students graduate with their Ph.D.s? What kind of message is this sending to young black women who want to have a career and a family? And why is this kind of thinking never directed at any of the male graduate students? It was then that I truly understood how black women in academia—be they faculty or administrators—must constantly fight two battles: (1) the battle against racism and (2) the battle against sexism. I can only imagine how different things would have been if I had a mentor who already had what I was trying to achieve—a mentor who was a black female, married, and a mother. Someone who "had it all" and did not have to choose between her professional aspirations and familial desires.

And Baby Makes 3 . . . and 4 . . . and 5 . . .

I think back to when I was in graduate school and pregnant with my son. Derrick and I decided that it was "time" to get started having a family. Actually I had to convince him that there would never be a perfect time and that, although I was in school, I was ready to begin our family. Here is another time that I would have benefited from having an older black female to mentor me in navigating this important part of my professional development. By this time, there was a second black female in our department who I became very close to, but she was newly married and junior faculty at that. However, she did help me get over my feelings of apprehension at telling my advisor that I was pregnant. In the end, my advisor was supportive, but I still believe that it would have been such a positive experience to be able to hear someone say, "you know, I was in the same position, and, as a black female, I want to tell you how to balance and navigate this experience while keeping it all in perspective." While I did have the support of family and friends, I know that having a mentor similar to me would have made it an easier path.

By the time my second child arrived, I had been employed at a small, private, liberal arts college for one year. But this time was different. I had a husband who had left the field of nursing to enter medical school. We left Columbus and settled in northeast Ohio (Kent to be exact). By that time, I had completed all of my coursework for my Ph.D. and was beginning to study for my general exams, but I was also suffering from severe burnout. Dealing with the politics of Ohio State and what I felt was a less than supportive environment for students with families had soured me on graduate school. I had NO DESIRE to become a faculty member. Thinking back, I know that if we would have stayed in Columbus, I would have eventually finished my degree but not because I wanted it. Instead, it would have been because I was there and had nothing else to do. Balancing work, marriage, and family was even more of a challenge now that we were away from family and friends. Sleep? What was that? Relax? When did I have time? Finish my Ph.D.? It just didn't seem like an option at the time. God, how I wish I would have tried to complete it at the time, even with the distance of two hours between Akron and Columbus. It would have been difficult, but it is only now that I realize, and grudgingly admit to myself, that it probably would have been easier then when life was only proceeding at 110 mph, instead of the 220 mph that I struggle with today.

There are times when I see young black females, much like myself, and get a little envious that they have their Ph.D.s or are completing theirs. In the past, I would never admit this envy to anyone, not even my husband. To do so would make me think, "maybe I really can't have it all; it's just too hard being a working mom and caretaker of the home and family. How can I even think of finishing school when I can barely get dinner on the table in the evening?" Even my time in the choir at church had to be put on hold after the birth of my last child. "If I can't make time for the choir," I thought, "what makes me think I can make time for school?"

Wise and Trusted Counselors—One Is Never Enough . . .

When did it become clear to me that I might want to finish by Ph.D.? Let me backtrack. When I was at my last job, my associate dean was a black female about the same age as my mother. She, herself, was a single parent when she was younger and in college, and with the support of her parents, she graduated from college and went on to graduate school, eventually working in the public sector and spending the last 10 to 15 years in higher education. One thing she always did was make me realize that, as a black woman, I could be that proverbial superwoman; it would just be a little harder. This was the first time in all of my years of school and work that I had a professional black woman who could fully speak to me and understand what I was going through. Finally, there was a female mentor telling me that this is how she survived as a black woman working in a white institution and that this is what I needed to do to be successful. She even said that the people who taught her how to play the game were white men!

Here was another example of a professional black woman who did not have the benefit of a professional black woman to mentor her during her career. How wonderful it would be if every black woman had someone to mentor her. No wonder it is so difficult for sisters to be successful in the workplace without being labeled because of the prejudices of white America. While my mom would give me a shoulder to lean on when I got frustrated with life, my colleague gave me strategies of how to manage my two worlds. Up until this time, I had only had men assisting me in this capacity.

Even though my female mentors have been few, I have had two male mentors—not including Dr. Franklin—who have helped me realize that I can and should get that degree. They have also made me realize that having a family and a career is something that I should strive for. Only then can I truly do what God has laid out for me. Dr. P. Eric Abercrumbie has continued to be one of my biggest supporters, calling me "Dr. Reedus" on a regular basis. I realize now that he has done this to keep me mindful of what I am missing in my "bigger picture." He is the male role model I mentioned earlier who taught me the importance of knowing how to play the game, and just as important, how to be a role model for other blacks who follow behind me. My other mentor is Dr. Kenneth Durgans who has been like a politician, bringing up graduate school when I least want to talk about it and holding me accountable. But isn't that what a mentor is supposed to do? The American Heritage Dictionary defines a mentor as "a wise and trusted counselor or teacher" and both of these men have been that and more to me. As I reflect on my own path, I know that some things would have been different, maybe even easier if there would have been more opportunities for me to have that Professional Black Woman/Mother/Wife/Student as my mentor. That mentor could have told me, "I've been where you have been, and it's only temporary. Don't let the rough times deter you." It is for this very reason that I am so close to many of my students of color, especially the females. I want them to understand that there is a connection between family and career, and that the two can and do complement each other. I want them to look at me and know that I am a living example of how professional and personal obligations may be taxing, but as a black person, things will always be stressful. Those same stresses can be fulfilling.

And So We Begin . . . Again . . .

I have finally made the decision to "keep on keepin' on." I am in the process of getting together my materials to apply for readmittance to the Ph.D. program at Ohio State University. I recently spoke with one of my previous professors at Ohio State, and she is helping me map out my plan. She has already agreed to serve on my committee if need be. Hopefully the process will not be filled with too many road blocks. But even if they are present—and I am sure they will be—I feel better equipped to handle the challenges. I have a wider network of friends and colleagues in higher education than I had starting out. And I still have my "amen corner" in my ear, encouraging me every step of the way. God has brought me to a place where I feel comfortable with this decision. If I wait until life slows down, I might be too old to enjoy the fruits of my labor. But just as important, I know that it is up to me to be a mentor for some young black professional woman—not because I have to, but because I want to. I want other black women to believe that they can attain their master's or Ph.D. and also have a family. It may take a little longer, but anything worth having is worth the extra time and effort that is required. Yes, it is a lot to juggle, but it is worth it in the end. Just as many women came before me so that I could have my opportunities, I have a strong desire to do the same for those to come after me, especially my two daughtSers. I want them to always know that Superwoman was more than just a cartoon—that she was their mother.

Diary of a Superwoman

"Take a look at my life and see what I see...."
But if you did look at my life, what would you see?
I guess it would depend on your vantage point, and what I am to you....
But I know what my eyes see—and it is wondrous to behold.

Take a look at me and see...black woman—strong, determined, and proud.
Continuing the struggle of Sojourner Truth and Fannie Lou, but more to my heart,
Nancy Jane, Mattie Mae, and Rose Marie.
Realizing that while the burden of the world makes me the "mule of society,"
It is the heritage of womanhood that makes me the mother of society—and the mother of necessity.

Take a look at me and see...wife—a partner, a help meet, and a soul mate
Understanding that I am not the better half or the other half;
For God made me complete in His image—in and of myself.
But He also made me to "leave" and to "cleave" to carry out His perfect will.
Only when I realized I was complete could I compliment the one that was predestined for me, for while my heart planned my course, the Lord ordered my steps.

Take a look at me and see...sister–girlfriend—arguing over clothes and bathroom time;
Laughing over hairstyles, "your father and mother," "your folks," and "daddy Derrick."
Crying over family drama, "her attitude," or June 30, 1996.
Bonding over nieces and nephews, hopes and dreams, holidays and everydays.
We are more than sisters, we are sister–girlfriend—sisters by birth, girls by nature, friends by choice.

Take a look at me and see...mother—by birth or by surrogacy.
Motherhood is sacrifice, selfishness, and discipline.
It's listening to a "guess what I did" when your mind is awake, but your body is tired.
It's talking about your kids and their experiences to everyone, believing that they really care, but not caring if they don't because—how could they not?
It's being maternal to those you didn't birth, but loving them like they are your own.
Those who I have a duty to mother, but to me and my heart, a privilege that's all mine.
To watch them grow from freshman to graduates, as they call me "mom" and I answer without a thought, and to tell their stories to everyone, believing that they really care, but not caring if they don't because—how could they not?

Take a look at my life and see what I see....
See what I see as important to me....
Take a look at my life and see what I see....
See how you have become a part of me—and how it is all too wondrous to behold.

(Dedicated to God, my spouse, my family, my children, and my students.)

Terri M. Hurdle

Terri M. Hurdle is a doctoral student within the University of Cincinnati's Urban Educational Leadership Program. Prior to Miss Hurdle's return to the classroom, she served the University of Cincinnati through the African American Cultural and Research Center as the BASE (Brothers and Sisters Excelling) Program Coordinator, assisting the university in its mission of retention and matriculation of black students. Prior to her work at the University of Cincinnati, she spent three years at Xavier University (Cincinnati, Ohio), first as a graduate assistant then as a fulltime Program Coordinator.

Miss Hurdle is a native of Cincinnati, Ohio. She was raised by her grandmother Edith Marie Gentry who instilled within her a strong spiritual foundation and the belief that through education she could reach heights of great attainment. Miss Hurdle graduated from Xavier University in 1993 with a bachelor's degree in Political Science. She returned to Xavier in 1997 and earned a master's degree in Criminal Justice in 2000. It was at Xavier University that Miss Hurdle discovered her gift for working with students and her desire to assist them in reaching their goals. As a result, she began her pursuit of a career in higher education.

Miss Hurdle is very committed to her family and leadership responsibilities. Currently, she is an active member of New Prospect Baptist Church and a member of Sigma Gamma Rho Sorority, Inc. Miss Hurdle dedicates this story to the memory of her grandmother, mom (Harrietta), little brother Johnathan, her family, and her close friends.

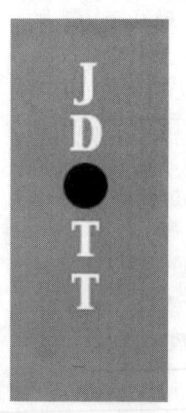

From Disappointment to Purpose: The Professional Progress of a Black Professional on a Predominantly White Campus

Terri M. Hurdle, M.S.

As a young child under the auspices of my grandmother (Mama), I can recall her utilizing different tactics to motivate me. They would range from a monetary reward, words of affirmation, or an inspirational speech. Her most prevalent tactic was the encouraging quote and/or scripture Phillipians 4:19, I can do all things through Christ which strengthens me. Statements such as "work hard and you will be successful," "the early bird catches the worm," and "if you ask, seek, and knock, the door will be opened" were stated quite often. In addition, who can forget "if you endure until the end, you shall receive your reward." Even though the aforementioned statements are true, my grandmother left out one component; they come with a price. The price can be in the form of lost relationships, taking on the responsibility of family members, or redirecting your dreams. Then as time continues to pass, it seems as if every opportunity slips through your fingers and the imaginary glass ceiling begins to close in on you. Suddenly, the confidence that was once personified in your stance starts to fade. As a result, your faith is shaken and just before you begin to break, you look for direction.

My senior year in high school reflected a number of changes in my life. On June 5, 1988, I formally graduated from Purcell-Marian high school in Cincinnati, Ohio. Praise the Lord! Through Him I had obtained a goal that had evaded both my mother and grandmother. Mama guided her professional career based upon an eighth grade education, while my mother, frustrated by a mental disability caused by an early accident, was limited academically. Yet, through it all, they both led me to my graduation. In addition, I was leaving Cincinnati in late August for Tuskegee University located in Alabama. I was on the move! My plans included graduating from Tuskegee with my bachelor's degree in four years and attending Howard Law School where I would be transformed into the next Barbara Jordan. After completing my scholarly work, I would move to Atlanta, marry my husband, and birth two to three kids by the time I was 25! Well, that was my dream and my vision at the age of 18 in 1988.

Fast-forwarding to 2004, the following has taken place: I graduated from Xavier University (Cincinnati, Ohio) with my B.A. in political science and masters in criminal justice. Currently, the University of Cincinnati employs me as a program coordinator where I assist the university in its mission of recruiting, retaining, and graduating black students. Finally, yet most importantly, my professional and educational goal now includes obtaining my doctorate in a program that is based upon the education of children in urban areas. How did I go from wanting to be a lawyer to being an educator? One might say that through my disappointments I found my Nia, one of the seven principles of Kwanzaa that is defined as purpose.

The Transition

When I was a small child, I, like other children, envisioned myself in different occupations such as a nurse, computer scientist, policewoman, etc. The issue was that the vision was there, but the belief in self was lacking. I suffered from low self-esteem, which stemmed from the fact that I lived in an urban area that was a slave to fashion. The majority of my clothes were hand-me-downs from my aunt, not to mention that I was a chubby girl and size 7 through 14 was not within my reach. Academically, I excelled in any subject that was associated with reading, but I had an anxiety attack when I had to study math and science.

To make matters worse, I had little support at home, not because my mother did not want to help, but because of her disability, she could not. At a very young age, my mother fell victim to an accident which had a major impact on her life. While visiting her great grandmother's farm, my mom swallowed soap lye. Unfortunately, no one knew that my mom had ingested the lye until it was too late. The lye affected her cognitive thinking ability and nervous system. Thus, my mom would lead the rest of her life with an ailment that would limit her learning ability.

My mother gave birth to me when she was 19 years old and maintained custodial care of me until I reached the age of 12. At the age of 12, she sent me to live with my grandmother, E. Marie Gentry. This was a major sacrifice for my mother. It was a major sacrifice for several reasons, the first being failure. In her mind, she was admitting to people that she could not handle raising a child. She also did not want to personify the image of an unfit parent. Last and certainly not least, I was her only child at that time and it hurt her to give me up. However, she felt that my grandmother was better equipped to instill in me a positive sense of self and Christian values. Upon my graduation from the sixth grade, I left my mother to live with my grandmother. The environment I moved into was the exact opposite of my earlier life. I went from a single-parent home to a two-parent household, and I entered Cure' of Ars, which was the beginning of my private school education. Never in my life had I been around so many Sister Mary Janets and Brother Phillips. To my surprise, I began to excel in math and science; the main reason for this improvement was my grandmother. Yes, she only had an eighth grade education, but what she lacked in classroom ability, God revealed to her through divine wisdom and knowledge. In addition, the class size at Cure' of Ars was small enough so that I could receive the necessary time and attention to learn. After two years, I left Cure' of Ars and proceeded to Purcell-Marian High School, where I started to actually envisage myself in a formal classroom setting after high school, which was Tuskegee University.

The First Disappointment: Tuskegee University

In the late summer of 1988, accompanied by my grandparents, I left the safety of Cincinnati for the unknown, which was Tuskegee University. I was so hopeful and excited about the new challenges in my life, living on my own, meeting new people, and so forth. I fell in love with Tuskegee when I first stepped foot onto the campus and saw a sea of positive black people going to class and socializing. I had become acquainted with the school through a black college tour sponsored by a local church in Cincinnati. On that first visit, I encountered members of the university who stated that at Tuskegee "you will be more than a number; we will treat you like family." I also viewed my first step-show, courtesy of the men of Omega Psi Phi Fraternity, Inc. Thus, I was sold on attending school in Alabama.

As a first year student, I was required to arrive at the university 10 days before the start of classes for orientation. My grandparents remained with me for two days to ensure that all was well, and then they headed back to Cincinnati. That was when things started to unravel. Given that I was the first person in my family to attend college, I was on my own as it related to filling out the paperwork. The FAFSA form for a novice such as I was incredibly difficult to figure out but I did it, or at least I thought I did. When I went to the financial aid office to inquire why I received so little aid, I located an error on the form. I received Assistance to Dependent Children (ADC) throughout my childhood because my father was not in my life, and my mom received Social Securuity (SSI) for her disability. Thus, I was poor or "p" as my friends and I jokingly stated. In the column where I was responsible for listing my personal income, I had listed the ADC payments which made it seem as if I had an annual income of $2,400 a year. Once the mistake was corrected, I was told that I would not be receiving any more assistance because all of it had been given out. I was devastated beyond belief. However, after my meeting with financial aid, I met with another university staff person who provided information about a payment plan. In addition, I stayed in Nurses Home Residence Hall, and the caretaker of the building offer me a job cleaning the building. I was determined to remain at Tuskegee because completing my education there was a major part of my overall plan. As a result, I thought the options given to me were fine, and I was willing to do them. Next came registration, another foreign procedure

From Disappointment to Purpose

for me. While I was attempting to register, it was discovered that the university had erroneously input my social security number by one number. Thus, I was forced to wait until the following day to register. The next problem I encountered was in relation to my loan; it had not been processed, so I could not confirm my registration nor place myself in the payment program. Nevertheless, I was determined to remain at Tuskegee. As a result, I, along with a number of students, waited in line to see Mr. Pettigrew, a school officer who had connections related to funding. To make a long story short, I was given additional financial assistance. However, when my grandmother was finally consulted relating to my minor obstacles, she said it was time for me to come home. Her reasons for wanting me to come home stemmed from distance and her ability to assist me if another problem arose.

The trip home was long and hard. In fact, I cried the entire way home on that Greyhound bus. In my mind, I had let everyone down; this included my family, church, and last but not least, myself. I cried out to the Lord and asked, "Why are you taking away my dream!" His answer was, "You have some responsibilities at home that you have run away from!" My responsibilities were my mother and three-month-old brother. At a young age, I knew without anyone telling me that I would be responsible for my mother. My grandmother helped her because of me, and I knew as I grew older that I would soon be responsible for her and my little brother Johnathan.

My mom's disability made it hard for her to learn how to read and write, so out of frustration she stopped attending school. For the period of time that I lived with my mother, my grandmother completed all paperwork. As I grew older, I too learned how to fill out the necessary forms for school lunches, emergencies, and so forth. Those responsibilities laid the groundwork for my future. When I was leaving for Tuskegee, I was hoping to evade what I viewed as the hold life had presented me.

When I first came home from Tuskegee, I started working at a bagel shop in a local mall. I grew comfortable with this until my grandmother made a very direct statement regarding bettering my life and continuing my education. As a result, I opened up the yellow pages and called two local colleges, the University of Cincinnati (UC) and Xavier University, for admission materials. I chose to attend Xavier over UC because of Xavier's small class sizes and teacher-to-student ratio. In January of 1989, I enrolled at Xavier. I hated it because it was not Tuskegee. Now I was the only black face in a stream of white. To make matters worse, my grades reflected my attitude. I did not do well my first semester there. At that time, something occurred to me; my goal was to go to school, and I was in school. No, it was not my first choice, but either I would make the most of this experience or drop out. The latter was not an option. After I stopped pouting, I poured more of myself into my classwork and extra-curricular activities. Through the extra-curricular activities, I was able to meet people such as Debora Jones, now Jobe, who took me under her wing and encouraged me. I also met my Big Sister for Life, Teresa Hamilton, our office secretary who scolded me when I was wrong and provided support when I needed it. In August of 1993, I graduated from Xavier University with a Bachelor of Arts in Political Science. I had achieved my first goal; I received my bachelors. Now law school?

Too Comfortable

After graduation, I started working at Great American Life Insurance Company as an annuities specialist. My initial plan was to work for a year and pay the remaining balance on my school bill. However, one year turned into four. My annual salary that first year was $18,500. This small amount of money paid my immediate bills that I had accumulated in college. Two years later I purchased my first car and started amassing new debt, which made the one-year position a necessity. I soon became complacent with my lifestyle even though I really was not happy. In addition, I had a supervisor who was neither supportive nor encouraging when related to work. At the insurance company, we had quotas and deadlines to maintain, and the vast majority of the time I maintained them. However, one day I made a mistake with a policy which caused me to be demoted. My supervisor called me into her office and gave me the news. She tried to make it seem as if it were not a bad thing, but I knew. She also let me know that my salary would follow me into my new position. As I packed my desk, I again began to harbor thoughts and feelings of inadequacy and resentment. At no point did my supervisor come to me and provide any type of direction that would assist in my improvement. Yet, when I really started thinking about the situation, I blamed myself. And so, I moved into the accounting position. The one good thing about the move was that it pushed me out of my comfort zone. I started taking a few courses at the University of Cincinnati and began reviewing UC's graduate programs. However, through a new friend and sorority sister, Stacy Downing, I also started researching the criminal justice program at Xavier University.

Starting Over

I started college again in the late summer of 1997, this time in Cincinnati and in a familiar place—Xavier University. I happily resigned my position at Great American and took a job at Xavier within the Office of Multicultural Affairs as a graduate assistant. My new plan included completing my master's degree and then proceeding to law school. However, something happened that made me question the earlier vision I had for my life. Miss Rosemary McCullough, the director of the Office of Multicultural Affairs, resigned from her position. As a result, the office now employed only two graduate assistants and a secretary. We had to pull together that year to produce programs and services for the students. At the end of the year, we were given a small award from the university for going beyond our responsibilities. After a year, Xavier hired Mila P. Cooper from Capital University as the office's new director. Mila took the office into a new direction. In addition to the mentor program, we added a program called Smooth Transitions, an orientation program for black students. The Office also assisted in revamping the Black Student Association and supported students' interest in historically black greek letter organizations. Through the above experiences, I started to grow. Mila came to me one day and asked, "Do you realize that you have a gift—working with students?" She deduced this because I spent a great deal of time advising, counseling, and working with students. Students sought me out on a daily basis. As a result, she negotiated with the university, and they committed to a new, one-year position within the office. I was now a program coordinator for the Office of Multicultural Affairs.

From Disappointment to Purpose

After a year at this position, I left Xavier University because my position was not renewed due to a hiring freeze. I was out of work for five months. I had a small, part-time job as an assistant manager at Lane Bryant which kept a roof over my head but barely paid my car payments. However, I was a person who believed in the "by any means necessary" philosophy. If getting by meant cleaning someone's home, I did it. If it meant running errands, I did it. My family knew nothing of my struggles because I did not share it with them. In addition, that same year my grandmother's ovarian cancer returned, shortening her time on earth. The full weight of being caretaker of my mom and brother was now coming to fruition. I was already managing my mother's finances and assisting with the upbringing of my brother, who was diagnosed as being mentally handicapped, although we later discovered that he was autistic. The year 2000 was a major struggle for me. My driving force during that period was my faith in God. Although I could no longer consult with my grandmother, she had given me the knowledge and scriptures that I could consult. As a result, I did a great deal of praise and worship in my small apartment.

One day Stacy Downing, assistant director of the African American Cultural and Research Center, called me concerning an open position of BASE (Brothers and Sisters Excelling) Program Coordinator at her office. They wanted me to interview for the position because I had facilitated a workshop for BASE and the director, Dr. P. Eric Abercrumbie (Doc), thought I did a good job. As a result, when the position became vacant, they called me. After interviewing with the director and assistant directors, I started work at the University of Cincinnati in October of 2000. During the same month, my grandmother left this life to be present with the Lord; one aspect of my life was ending while another was beginning.

My first year at UC went well, thank God! I, along with my BASE Steering Committee, increased the attendance at the weekly workshops, and students really enjoyed their time in a first-year experience program called Transitions. At this point in my life, I thought I was ready for another challenge. I maintained the role of program coordinator for the past three years. Even in my role as the graduate assistant at Xavier, I functioned as a program coordinator. A new position entitled Assistant Director of Multicultural Affairs was posted at Xavier University within my old office. When I saw the position, I thought this was an excellent opportunity for me. I had already decided that leaving Cincinnati was not an option. My mother and brother were my responsibility, so I would have to look for professional opportunities within the tri-state area. After applying for the position at Xavier, I discovered that a university colleague had also applied for the position. I was one of two candidates who Xavier wanted to fill the position; the other prospect was my UC colleague. Xavier offered her the position. I was shocked and distressed. How did I lose this position? I put so much time, energy, and hope into this process. With this position I could have provided for my mom and little brother with little effort. Hadn't I paid my dues? As I looked around, I saw people succeeding who did not do as much as I, who were not as faithful as I. I was angry with God. He had made me all these promises that were not being fulfilled. At that point I stopped praying. I said "forget it." I did it God's way and all I had received was disappointment after disappointment. God had placed many hurdles in my life, and I was getting over them. However, this time I did not have the energy to do so. Doc saw the change in my attitude and he took me aside and had a discussion with me. For the first part of our conversation, I was resistant. Then I let my guard down and cried. Those tears played an early role in my healing process. The next thing I did was accept my current situation; I was where God wanted me to be. I also did some interpersonal reflection and moved onto my next challenge, law school.

My family, mostly my Uncle Daryl, continued to push me toward law school. In addition, one of my sorority sisters thought this was the best way for me to make more money. I pursued law school, but because of my low-test scores I did not gain entry. When I was denied admittance, I took it in stride, and I actually sat down and really investigated where I should be professionally. The road led me to education. I saw myself in a role where I could be a facilitator, teacher, and motivator. The most important thing was that I saw myself being sincerely happy with my life. As a result, I am pursuing a doctoral program, working with local schools and enjoying my current position.

One of my favorite songs is "I'm Still Here" by Dorinda Clark-Cole. In one line of the song, she reflects over her life and she states, "I would have never made it this far but through disappointments; the Lord has brought me through." My disappointments navigated me to my purpose, which is education. Looking back, the answer was always there, but I ignored it. For those of you going through anything loosely similar to my situation, my advice is take a step back, look at your disappointments, and move towards your purpose.

Ryan J. Davis

Ryan J. Davis is currently a graduate fellow at the Institute for Higher Education Policy and a Ph.D. student in the Higher Education Program at the University of Maryland, College Park. Mr. Davis has previous administrative experiences in the areas of summer bridge programs, admissions, housing and residential life, career services, and student service administration. He is actively involved in undergraduate level instruction, professional associations and university service, research and policy analysis, and mentoring and advising students.

Mr. Davis earned a B.S. in Business Administration from Eastern Connecticut State University, where he was awarded the Dr. Martin Luther King Distinguished Service Award. He then went on to earn an M.S.Ed. in Higher Education Administration from Old Dominion University, where he was awarded the Outstanding Graduate Student in Higher Education Award and the Emerging Professional Award.

Some of Mr. Davis's specific engagements include service on the National Advisory Committee for the National Conference on Race and Ethnicity; the Editorial Board for the *Journal of College and University Student Housing*; a mentor for Upward Bound; and a regular presenter at the American College Personnel Association, the National Association of Student Personnel Administrators, and the National Conference on Race and Ethnicity. His research interests include assessing the impact of early intervention and retention programs on students of color, particularly Latino and African-American men, and the effects institutional and public policies have on college students from disadvantaged groups, namely those from low-income backgrounds.

On the Road to Success: Helping Low-Performing African-American Male Undergraduates Become High Achievers

Ryan J. Davis, M.S.Ed.

At this time in my life, I must say that I would not rather be doing anything else, anywhere else. Being young, healthy, spiritual, and progressing toward completing the doctorate of philosophy (Ph.D.) degree at a top-tier institution naturally enables me to count my blessings each day and continuously provide opportunities that I have been afforded to other students whenever the opportunity permits, especially among African-American male undergraduates on predominantly white campuses. I am passionate about devoting my time and resources to this particular group in this particular context because the interplay between black men and white campus climates are often incongruent.

Along with my own happiness and contentment, my relatives, friends, parents, and mentors are also proud of my progress and current path to success. Local newspaper reporters in close proximity to my alma mater frequently contact me to discuss and subsequently quote my success in a summer bridge program and college experience for their press releases. I now have become one of "the few who are doing something with their lives" among my same-race peers from high school. I say this because, immediately after I graduated from Windsor High School, I would often hear my peers' gossip about graduates (and non-graduates) who took unfortunate paths and made decisions that did not complement their potential for success. Far too often, I would hear the popular ladies man, class diva, and promising superstar athlete in high school ending up formally unemployed, selling drugs, and never aspiring to earn any form postsecondary educational certificate or degree. This has been troublesome for me to hear because in the postindustrial global era, a high school diploma no longer assures one a decent job or even a livable wage (Nembhard, 2005). Now, I am glad to be dissimilar to my peers who are the talk of unpleasant news, but during my high school years I did anything to affiliate myself with this group. Now don't get me wrong, I was popular in high school. In fact, I was selected as "King" for our senior semi-formal dance, won the "Most Attractive" superlative award, and was an "All Conference" baseball player. My problem was that I changed my own personality and social norms to conform to the socially accepted image that my peers made up. This conformity would continue through high school and had a direct effect on my level of academic focus and desire to achieve excellence in all capacities because I disliked my own self-image. Consequently, no one—including myself—articulated an expectation of me getting accepted into any college or university; therefore, those involved in my life planned more carefully for alternative career options that eventually seemed to mismatch with my desired income level and career trajectory.

With the help of my parents, however, I fortunately beat the odds and enrolled in higher education. Subsequently, I got involved in numerous out-of-class activities and capitalized on meaningful relationships, which directly affected my academic ability, drive, and motivation to succeed. More specially, these interactions helped me progress toward attaining a bachelor's degree and then immediately pursuing two graduate degrees.

Through this process, I went from being considered a low-performing student to a high-achieving student. I should make clear that my self-identified transition from a low-performer to a high-achiever was only after overcoming several social and academic problems in high school and college.

I invite you to listen closely to my story as I tell you how these problems were identified and how I overcame them. This anecdote can be very important for higher education professionals who wish to understand the way in which meaningful relationships can significantly impact African-American male college student achievement. To this end, there are many benefits of familiarizing oneself with this topic, but the crowning purpose of my story is to illustrate how giftedness and high-achievement among African-American men can be a developmental process as opposed to an innate quality. As I attempt to meet this objective, I will also provide recommendations for campus officials, parents, and students to help African-American males (1) identify their strengths or gifts, (2) capitalize on their strengths to become successful in college through different forms of engagement, and (3) identify and avoid some of the barriers that often prevent success among African-American male undergraduates.

Review of Literature

A large body of research exists on the plight of African-American males in higher education and society at large. While this work has been insightful, it does not demonstrate what all African-American men symbolize nor have potential of representing. Several studies (Bonner, 2001; Bonner, 2003; Ford, Harris, Tyson, and Trotman, 2002; Freeman, 1999; Fries-Britt, 1997; Fries-Britt, 1998; Fries-Britt, 2000; Fries-Britt, 2002; Harper, 2005; Hrabowski, Maton, and Greif, 1998) have begun to change this pattern of discourse and focus on gifted African-American undergraduates and some of the climate issues this high-achieving group encounters on predominantly white campuses. A number of the problems that exist surrounding gifted African-American collegians, which include feelings of same-race isolation (Ford, et al., 2002; Fries-Britt, 1998), racial identity issues (Fries-Britt, 2000), and detrimental peer-to-peer relationships as barriers to their success (Guiffrida, 2004), call for increased attention to investigate these issues more closely. More importantly, suggestions to reverse these experiences are needed to promote the achievement of African-Americans. In response to these issues, the authors of these articles offered some practical recommendations for professionals to support this group. These suggestions include effective mentoring services or programs (Freeman, 1999; LaVant, Anderson, and Tiggs, 1997), active engagement in out-of-class activities (Guiffrida, 2003; Harper, 2005), encouraging active family involvement in the educational process to enhance student achievement (Ford, et al., 2002; Hrabowski, et al., 1998; Fries-Britt, 1997), and establishing a safe place to group high-achieving African-American students together so the perception of being gifted and black will be viewed as normal (Fries-Britt, 1998). Identifying these issues and recommendations to improve college life for gifted African-American students becomes just as important for those black students who have the potential to become high-achievers but have not had the resources or even realized their own strengths. Oftentimes, the talents of these students have remained untapped and it simply requires campus administrators, parents, and peers to utilize these recommendations to accentuate students' giftedness.

The authors in the studies above have provided a solid foundation on this topic and do an excellent job of highlighting the positive experiences of high-achieving African-American students and the resources they need to succeed. However, only some of the studies focus on African-American male undergraduates specifically and none of this research tells us how these students actually became high-achievers. While it may not have been in the scope and purpose of their studies to share this information, ignoring this phenomenon completely may leave the assumption that being gifted, black, and male is an innate quality (Freeman, 1999) versus a process. Additionally, most of the methodologies that these researchers employed depict the voices of groups of students. Certainly, listening to the rendering of one black man's anecdote on how he became a high-achieving African-American male student would provide a unique insight and more depth to this type of scholarship.

Rewinding to My Childhood

To further clarify how the aforementioned summary of my life after high school and review of literature relates to my story, I will take you back to my childhood to discuss my academic inability to succeed and struggle with racial identity development. I will also discuss how peer influences affected my enrollment in developmental education courses throughout high school and admitted to college only under the condition that I participate and successfully complete a summer bridge program. Then, you will hear about the meaningful relationships that I made with campus officials and other supporting collegians, which not only increased my drive and motivation to succeed, but also provided the necessary resources for me to become a high-achieving African-American male student and ultimately be in high demand at several top-tier Ph.D. programs of Higher Education Administration. Learning about my sociocultural and psychosocial development has several implications for professionals to influence African-American male students in a progressive direction by creating meaningful relationships on predominantly white campuses. To this end, I invite concerned professionals to take these implications seriously if there is an espoused commitment to enrich the social and academic campus climate among African-American male undergraduates on your campus.

Reflecting on my upbringing, I must say that my sister and I have lived a very privileged life. Everything we needed and most of what we wanted was at our fingertips. In my opinion, the only stigma that made my parents one notch under perfection was their divorce when I was three years old. Being raised on the notion that my sister and I should always stick together and take care of one another regardless of anything that happens, their decision to divorce became a hypocritical action in my eyes. My parents' separation was very painful for me up until the age of 13. Now that I am older and have been exposed to the realities of the "real world," I recognize their personal situation and understand their choice to divorce was indeed the best decision for the family. Thus, as I matured into my teenage years and to the present day, I continue to hold my parents in the highest regard.

After my parents divorced, my father moved to the city of Hartford, Connecticut—the state capital and also his birthplace. Meanwhile, I grew up with my mother and sister in Windsor, Connecticut, which is the neighboring town to Hartford. Windsor primarily consists of two socio-economically and racially segregated groups. The families that reside closer to the city are predominantly African-American families with lower household incomes and those who live deeper in the suburbs are primarily white families with much higher incomes. I, without any regret, grew up in the predominantly white side of town and attended a predominantly white public elementary school. Although my sister and I were exposed to minimal racial/ethnic diversity as children, we both received excellent public educations and never experienced any racist encounters or felt marginalized growing up. However, being raised around mostly white children made it more difficult for me to process my own racial identity once I advanced to middle school, which consisted of more racially/ethnically diverse students. Although I deem my elementary school education above average, my grades were not. I always had academic difficulty and would often daydream about the things I enjoyed, such as playing baseball and admiring girls in my class.

Since kindergarten, I had always been considered a mediocre student and was threatened on one occasion with repeating a grade if I did not catch up with the rest of my classmates. My older sister, on the other hand, was one who I would identify as naturally gifted—a bright student who enjoyed learning for learning's sake and who consistently received above average grades. I hated when report cards were sent home because, on my part, there was always a subconscious comparison between the grades my sister and I received. Unfortunately for me, there were large gaps in our success. While she brought high honor roll stickers, I recall being happy if I earned a C+ letter grade. My parents always adored her for continuously earning her way on the honor role and playing the clarinet. My sister was like many older siblings and picked on me whenever possible. To make matters worse, my father regarded her as his "number one" for a long time, which chipped away at my ego and self-confidence. Finally, when I was about 10 years old, I confronted him about the favoritism he often showed toward my sister by calling her his "number one" child all the time. I asked him "Dad, when will I ever be number one?" He thought to himself, rationalized, and articulated to me that he was saying this because my sister was born first. He quickly realized, however, that calling me his "number two" child psychologically contributed to my low self-esteem and low confidence. When he realized the impact this had on me, he immediately acted upon his mistake by putting me in the front seat and referring to my sister as his "number one daughter" and to me as his "number one son." Of course my sister, who loved to have all the attention, hated this change. For me, it was a first step that shifted my self-image towards higher self-esteem and self-confidence.

Although my father and I resolved that labeling issue, my struggles with my self-perception continued through middle school and in early high school. These years were filled with difficulties of "fitting in," which included trying to incorporate slang words into my speech, being a virgin, fearing relations beyond friendship with the opposite sex, and falling short of remaining abreast with the most current fashion trends. Perhaps my suburban upbringing contributed to the misfit I experienced during my secondary educational experience. Academically, I was seriously lacking fundamental mathematics, science, and reading skills, and it became difficult for me to comprehend what was actually being taught. In seventh grade, I was tested for a learning disability. As a result of several assessments, I was diagnosed with some form of Attention Deficit Disorder and was placed in a developmental education program that allowed students extra time to complete class assignments and tests. The program also gave students individual, one-on-one attention to help them break down the meaning of the directions and provided tutorial assistance as well. Although I knew this program provided me with the fundamental tools I needed to progress through my secondary school curriculum, I always felt ashamed and stupid for being placed in this program because most of my "friends" were in intermediate courses. To fit in with many of my peers, it seemed like I had to dig my way out of the developmental program, but not excel past them into a curriculum designed specifically for honors students.

These feelings were all my issues, but at that time, I perceived them to be controlled primarily by my peers due to their negative view of anything outside of mediocrity. During that same time, I quickly became an easy target to be "ranked on" for wearing non-name-brand clothing because I was unfamiliar with the fashion trends in early high school. This became extremely hurtful and drove my confidence level to an all-time low. During this same period in my life, my sister, who was two grades ahead of me, was academically and socially integrated with both high-achieving and popular students. She accomplished this by earning a spot on the honor role each semester, having the most popular and "promising" rap star in the town as her boyfriend, and winning the hearts of all my friends who wanted to date her. Though she recollects being teased at times for her smartness, it was more socially accepted for girls to be placed in honors classes as opposed to boys. Even more depressing times occurred for me when my sister's friends, who were two years older than me, joked on me for not having hit puberty at age 13. Simply reflecting on these experiences still brings back the painful memories of my childhood.

By the time I entered my sophomore year in high school, I began to "learn the game." I did the things that pleased everyone else, which in turn gave me the satisfaction of fitting in with my peers. I developed a complete name-brand wardrobe with shirts, jeans, and shoes made by Polo-Ralph Lauren, Nautica, Tommy Hilfiger, Timberland, and Nike Air. I am sure that these designers appreciate the support even more than my high school peers. By my junior year in high school, I became more interested in the latest fashions and received more positive attention from my peers. Although I changed and became a new person, I was more socially satisfied because I felt more in tune with black culture at my high school.

During this period, my father noticed that I was changing my behaviors and beginning to follow the wrong crowd. We would often argue about the things we did not like about one another. I always said that I hated his cigarette-smoking and alcohol-drinking habits and he would often tell me I was being a "follower" for choosing friends that cared more about their image than the well being of their friends. I hated to hear this, and at the time, I completely disagreed. I saw it as becoming one of the few leaders that were admired and respected in- and outside of school. Now I can clearly see his points and we often have long talks about how that impacted our father-son relationship. A time when I really let my father down was in the summer prior to my senior year in high school. In June of 1998, there was a huge concert coming to town featuring L. L. Cool J. A few months before the actual concert, I was talking about it all the time and told my father I wanted to go. My father, who has a side profession of photography, received complimentary passes to these types of events as part of his work, so as soon as I articulated an interest in attending, he was able to obtain four tickets. Of course, I chose the top four "friends" who I thought would enhance my image. I knew this would be a perfect opportunity for my other peers to see me grouped with a popular set of guys, which would enhance my own image. Once the concert came around, I was feeling good. I had my shades on with a smooth swagger. Before the concert began, my "friends" and I were in the lobby waiting for the concert to begin. Suddenly, my father (who had a mini afro, a potbelly, wore a white Hanes t-shirt, Khaki shorts, and sandals) approached me and my three "friends" and asked if he could take a group picture. As he was approaching us, one of my "friends" said under his breath, "look at this cat. This dude looks like the guy off Sanford and Son." While the other two guys laughed, I disregard the comment by not mentioning this was my father and ended up taking the picture with them. Right after the picture was taken, my father approached me for hug, but I denied him. I would later find out that my action hurt him very much. This action would suggest many things to him, but one thing that stood out was that I chose my "friends" over him—my own father. Indeed my "friends" were happy to have their photo in one of the city's newspapers, but I was too ashamed to tell them my father, the person who placed us there, was the man who took the picture. As I matured and even to this day, my father and I sit and talk about the psychosocial experiences I encountered to justify that I was indeed an excellent follower. Today, reflecting on my actions on that day simply leaves me in self-disgust.

As my relationship with my father further developed while I was in high school, I began to improve academically and was no longer placed in developmental courses. Now in intermediate classes, I felt better about myself and I was able to fit in with most of my peers. Socially, I remained the same and continued to do the things that impressed my peers; however, I did eliminate some so called "friends" who did more harm to me than good. By the time I was in my senior year in high school, I realized that graduation was fast approaching and had to make some choices about my life and career. I ended up completing high school as an average student, earning mostly Cs. My parents always let me know that they loved me dearly and discussed the possibility of attending college, but they did not articulate a clear expectation for me to actually enroll due to my lack of drive and motivation to succeed academically. Therefore, there was never any pressure on me to apply to college. However, having aspirations of playing baseball and one day becoming a chief executive officer of a Fortune 500 company, I knew that I had to attend college to achieve these goals.

My College Experience

Recognizing my low academic achievement and the influence my peers had over me, I wanted to apply to an institution that was close enough to home that my parents could provide encouragement and support but far enough away to restrict me from being able to come home every weekend and be distracted by my hometown friends. I applied to two medium sized, public, state universities in Connecticut—Central Connecticut State University (CCSU) and Eastern Connecticut State University (ECSU). With a considerably low grade point average (GPA) and even worse Standardized Academic Test (SAT) scores, I had very little expectations of being accepted anywhere. Not to my surprise, I was rejected by CCSU, but I was surprised to be conditionally admitted into ECSU. ECSU was my first choice because of their nationally recognized Division III baseball team, as well as my father's connection and friendship with Mr. Floyd Bagwell, the director of the Learning Center at ECSU. I was enthused about enrolling at ECSU, but I did not know what to expect.

Being conditionally accepted into ECSU meant that I had to enroll in a six-week summer precollege program called the Summer Transition Program at Eastern/Contract Admissions Program (STEP/CAP) that was housed under the Learning

Center, which is the office Mr. Bagwell directs. Participants in STEP/CAP were required to take entry-level and remedial college courses, and they also received a full year of administrative and tutorial support upon successful completion of the summer program. All students had to earn at least a 2.0 GPA to successfully matriculate into the fall semester. I was looking forward to attend this program to get a head start on my coursework and adjust to college life.

To this day I still vividly remember my time in STEP/CAP. My time was consumed with studying, socializing, and going to class with the other 59 participants so the six weeks in this program flew by rather quickly. Although I barely passed STEP/CAP with a 2.28 GPA, the program was indeed a helpful adjustment to academic and social college life.

In the fall semester of my freshman year, I made two choices that set me back. First, I met a group of "friends" who were from the north part of Hartford, Connecticut, which is a low socioeconomic but respected area by African-Americans from my hometown. Since we lived in the same residence hall, we hung out just about every night trying to meet new people, namely females. Secondly, I joined the ECSU baseball team during my first semester. A college administrator warned me that students of color who had played on the team in the past had experienced some mistreatment. However, with a deep love for baseball and never having experienced any racial mistreatment growing up, I overlooked his comment and fully committed myself to the baseball team. Practice was twice a day for three hours, six days a week. Playing baseball at this level became more like a job than a game. Hanging out with my black "friends" at night and white "friends" on the baseball field left me exhausted and too tired to study and complete homework assignments.

Before I knew it, mid-semester grades became available. The STEP/CAP program was designed in a way to monitor students' progress through the first year. I knew my grades were poor and I was very reluctant to attend my mid-semester review meeting with the STEP/CAP staff, especially with Mr. Bagwell. I recall this meeting lasting approximately 30 minutes; yet I do not remember much of what was said. In fact, with the whole staff of nine surrounding me in the conference room, the only thing I clearly remember is Mr. Bagwell asking; "You don't want me to have to tell your father about your grades, do you?" When he said this, my eyeballs expanded, blood pressure rose, and heart fluttered. Although my father was never abusive, I always feared him. I could tell Mr. Bagwell was very serious about making this phone call so I nervously shook my head when he made this comment and said, "No," with hope that he would never contact my dad regarding my poor grades. I really made a concentrated effort to improve my academic standards after that meeting.

The day after the meeting, at a baseball game, our best pitcher was scheduled to start, meaning that he was the first to pitch in that game. The relief pitchers, those who may come in the game later, were resting in the dugout. On this particular day, there had been a rain delay and the field was significantly wet. As the starting pitcher was warming up, he told me to go rake the bullpen. At first I looked at him in a confused state of mind, primarily because the coach, who typically gave orders, was right next to him. However, I quickly put the confusion behind me and raked the muddy bullpen and drained the puddles to the best of my ability. With the weather being very cool and dense, it was impossible to turn the mud into smooth ground before the game was scheduled to begin. After the starting pitcher warmed up in the bullpen, he sprinted back to the dugout where I and the other relieving pitchers were. He then got in my face and screamed, "What the f*!k are you good for? You can't even rake a f%@king bullpen! You piece of sh$t!" As he was screaming at me, my emotions began to flare. I was thinking, "After I helped this guy get ready for his start, he blatantly disrespected me in front of our teammates and coach." I wanted to punch him in his face, but I assumed that the coach was going to handle the situation and immediately reprimand him in some way. As the coach turned his back to the situation, I realized that I needed to do something. Although I wanted to hit my teammate with a baseball bat, I did not. I made sure that the coach was aware of the situation. The coach heard me out and said he would talk to the starting pitcher. It was evident that I was looking for the problem to be resolved immediately; however, no action took place. As the game began, foul balls were hit and it was the non-starting pitchers' job to fetch the baseballs. As balls went into foul territory, the coach was always ordering me to fetch them rather than other nonstarting white pitchers. Given that the situation between the starting pitcher and I was not resolved, I refused to take any further orders. The coach asked me, "What's your problem? If you don't want to be here, then you can leave!" This is when I walked off the field and left the game I loved behind. Although no direct racial terminology was used against me in this situation, this attack along with other previous degrading situations that occurred in practice made me realize that the administrator who warned me of experiences that students of color typically have on the team was accurate.

Now, with more time on my hands, I began to prepare for classes, study harder, and I sought extra help in the classes in which I struggled. However, I still hung out every night with the same group of "friends" that had a priority of smoking, drinking, and partying every night of the week. Unfortunately, I did not recognize that following my "friends" were detrimental to my academic and professional success. After my roommate had sex with my girlfriend from Hartford, I realized that these people were not my true friends.

With baseball and my former "friends" behind me, the only thing I had to do now was my coursework. By this time it was mid November and I felt as if ECSU was not the place for me. Just a few days later, on a cold and snowy day when I was riding the shuttle bus to class, an elderly white woman got onto the bus when all the seats were taken. I quickly offered my seat to the woman and stood up for the remainder of the ride. An older ECSU student, Ron Bernard, noticed my mannerisms and complimented me on my kindness. Ron said, "That was very nice of you to give your seat up. You know, you're the type of brother we need in our organization—Men Achieving Leadership, Excellence, and Success (M.A.L.E.S.)." At first I was skeptical because I never viewed myself as one to get involved in campus life outside of baseball. However, after thinking about it for a week or so, I decided to attend a M.A.L.E.S. meeting. Before I knew it, I was a full member and was bonding with other black men who participated in community service activities, leadership development, fundraising, and mandatory study halls. I connected with these men in a different way from my previous friends and became very focused on excellence in everything I did.

Mr. Tarome Alford, who was a mentor and the advisor of M.A.L.E.S., as well as my peers within the organization, would eventually encourage me to become more involved in campus activities. I ended up obtaining a resident assistant (RA) position, an internship with the director of Career Services, and a hall director position for the 2002 STEP/CAP program, which is the program that I participated in and that became the foundation of my success. My everyday attire began to change from urban street wear to collared shirts, ties, and dress slacks. This was largely due to the dress requirements of working in Career Services with Mr. Diaz, who mentored me on professionalism, ethics, effective writing techniques, relationships, and job search strategies. I was well-known by student affairs administrators and began earning 3.0 GPAs each semester. By my senior year in college, I was awarded the Dr. Martin Luther King, Jr., Distinguished Service Award and the Resident Assistant of the Year Award. As I reached this level of achievement, I realized that the turning point in my success began with the continued support I received from Mr. Bagwell and the Learning Center staff as a result of my participation in STEP/CAP.

By this time, I could now easily be identified as a high-achieving African-American male student. When I first started college, I planned my coursework to graduate in five years. After I got involved and connected with positive black men, I remained enrolled all year, including the summer, fall, winter, and spring terms, to graduate in four. During my final semester, I was taking 21 credits and holding an internship in Career Services. I also was promoted to a Senior RA, held an executive board position with M.A.L.E.S., searched for jobs, and applied to graduate school. With all this activity, I was still able to earn a 3.2 GPA in that same semester. In sum, I must admit that being mentored, my involvement with M.A.L.E.S., having peer support from other high-achieving black men, and on-campus employment positively shaped my development and overall success.

Putting It All into Perspective

There were many heartaches' as a result of being "ranked on," attempting to process my racial identity, identifying as a student with a learning disability who was placed in developmental education courses, being admitted to college on a conditional basis, and struggling academically throughout my early years in college. However, these experiences have given me strength and the ability to take control over my own successes and shortcomings. As I matured in college and capitalized on meaningful engagements with caring campus officials and peers I began to feel very blessed, privileged, successful. I attribute most of my success to supportive parents, effective mentorship, peer encouragement to succeed, and my aspiration to take advantage of the opportunities presented to me. Capitalizing on these engagements as an African-American male in a predominantly white environment helped me academically transcend from a low-performing student to a high-achieving student.

Now in graduate school I continue to capitalize on the lessons learned at ECSU. The more involved I become, the better I perform. Most recently I have been very active within professional associations and university service activities. I am also formally advising and mentoring students and teaching undergraduate courses. The lessons that I learned from capitalizing on meaningful engagements have been extremely helpful in my personal and professional development. As a result, I continue to employ this same strategy to continue to advance my career in a progressive and respected direction.

Additionally, reflecting on the positive outcomes associated with the gains I made on a predominantly white campus clarified my desire to pursue higher education administration as a profession. The personal gains I receive from assisting other students the same way I received assistance contributes to my unwavering passion to follow this career path. My hope is that learning from my experiences will help me continue to help other African-American male students for years to come.

Recommendations

In this story, I wrote about my own personal anecdote and exposed some of my most shameful and embarrassing moments in college. Moreover, you read about the struggles I encountered to become a high achiever and how the connections I made in college turned my life around to move toward success. Many college students have shared or will share a similar story with you. In order to be prepared for such an account, I offer you five important recommendations that are grounded in literature as well as blended with my personal experiences so that you, as a professional in academia are able to help reverse the potential of low-performing African-American male undergraduates and actually bring out the gifts that lie within them.

First, we must recognize, as my mentors have, that African-American men do not always perform at high levels due to various reasons, especially forms of peer pressure. Thus, those who are gifted may not necessarily be high-achievers. In fact, Ford and her colleagues (2002) assert that "When one equates gifted with high-achievement, gifted underachievers will not be recruited into gifted programs and their needs will be unrecognized and unmet (p. 7)." My contentment in developmental education courses as a result of peer influences throughout middle- and part of high-school brings clarity to this notion. Therefore, it becomes important for campus officials to reach out to African-American male students and recognize their full academic and leadership potentials. It is also equally important for African-American men to maintain good friends that will promote their academic successes as opposed to demoting it. Likewise, parents must continuously articulate academic high expectations for their children. The receipt of confidence and enthusiasm from parental figures is vital in African-American male self-perception of their own perceived worthiness. Hrabowski et al. (1998) also suggests that parents should have continuously high expectations, open, consistent, and strong communication. It is important to note that strong communication does not equate to verbal abuse. Rather, it's a form of strong cultural language that will help young black men carry themselves with pride and self-confidence as a black man in a predominantly white society. This communication style will also help create positive racial and gender identification.

Secondly, to increase students' level of comfort with high achievement, professionals should try linking potentially high-achieving students with other talented and gifted students to create an environment in which high-achievement is the norm. Not only is this phenomenon evident by way of my participation in the M.A.L.E.S. organization, but Fries-Britt (1998) also made clear that students who meet and study with other gifted black students inspire one another to study harder, which reduces insecurities of "acting white" and ultimately improves the campus climate for gifted black students.

Following this same thought, it is also important for African-American men to recognize when their peers are more of a liability than an asset. For a significant time period, my decision to be a follower of those who had different aspirations from mine significantly hindered my success. Guiffrida (2004) also found that friends from home might hinder African-American student's chances to become involved and socially integrated at predominantly white institutions. More specifically, the low-achievers interviewed in Guiffrida's study blamed their friends from home for their academic pitfalls while high-achieving students were able to identify and retain the peers who helped them succeed. These same high-achieving African-American students distanced themselves from those who had minimal interest in their success.

My third recommendation speaks more directly toward African-American male students than administrators. Rather than African-American male undergraduates focusing on retaining various friends from home, students should try building meaningful peer relationships with others who aspire to achieve similar goals. In Harper's (2004) article, "Inside the Experiences of High-Achieving African American Male Students" as well as my initial encounter with the former president of the M.A.L.E.S. organization, an older African-American male student encouraged the younger African-American male student to get involved. These two findings are perfect examples for campus administrators who wish to utilize their current student leaders to reach out to first-year African-American male students. The recruitment of African-American men in these activities is more likely to occur if there are groups specifically for African-American men. If there is not one, become responsible for creating one. For tangible examples of some successful programs, see Cuyjet's (2006) book, *African American Men in College.*

Fourth, creating or utilizing existing mentoring programs is also a key success factor for many African-American men. Mr. Bagwell, Mr. Alford, and Mr. Diaz chronologically came into my life at different time periods and noticed a young African-

American male with potential to succeed. Their dedication to help students like me advance continues to transform distraught African-American male students into competent and marketable emerging young professionals. The meaningful relationship these professionals make with students is needed to assist in the personal and academic development of African-American men on predominantly white campuses. Additionally, the correlation between my positive peer-to-peer relationships with the members of the M.A.L.E.S. organization obviously impacted my success. LaVant and his colleagues (1997) also highlight the importance of mentoring groups for African-American men in college. The mentoring models that were discussed include The Black Man's Think Tank, The Student African American Brotherhood, The Black Male Initiative, The Meyerhoff Program, The Bridge, and Project BEAM. Although same-race and gender mentors are significant in the role of guiding African-American male undergraduate success, it is certainly not the only way. In my situation, for example, Mr. Diaz, who is now my closest mentor, is Puerto Rican. Moreover, two out of the four advisor of M.A.L.E.S. in 2002 were white men. I should also mention two of my peers who recruited me to become an RA were white female seasoned RAs. This suggests that, in my situation, caring professionals and peers are more important than gender and race. A collection of committed professionals should ensure that programs begin as soon as students make contact with a college or university (Freeman, 1999). Lastly, if mentoring programs, such as the one mentioned above, that are designed to help African-American men succeed in college are of high priority, executive administration must genuinely be committed and allocate the staffing and financial resources to replicate or design similar programs (LaVant, et al., 1997).

Fifth, the influence of family is vital in the success of African-American students. For a significant portion of my life, I wanted to be equally appreciated and admired by my parents just like my sister. Clearly, my perceived lack of attention and appreciation took a huge toll on my happiness and self-confidence. However, I now realize that it was my own psychosocial developmental issues that hindered my progress. Now, for example, I would never deny my father a hug in front of anybody. In fact, I actually cherish the receipt of love given by my father as I have grown to recognize that he, as a black male father, is not common among black families in today's society. Similarly, Hrabowski et al. (1998) notes the importance of the parents' voice, particularly the father's voice in the father-son relationship. This was documented as significant in the development of academically successful African-American men. To this end, I suggest that finding African-American male students' talents and parents providing continuous positive reinforcement should always be given high priority. To capitalize on this, those campus administrators who are liaisons to parents should encourage student-parent engagement in the college process immediately upon a student's enrollment and all the way to graduation.

Summary and Conclusion

The gains I made from involvement and cultivating meaningful relationships suggests that African-American men as high-achievers can be a process, not just an attribute that one is born with. My story clearly illustrates the need and promotion for more meaningful engagements to occur for black men on predominately white campuses. With a heighten concern surrounding black men in college (Cuyjet, 2006), campus administrators should begin to "tap into" the gift that is within African-American men. This story and other research (Guiffrida, 2003; Harper, 2004; 2006) confirmed that facilitating campus involvement would certainly assist in black male social and academic development. As I have recommended, this is a three-fold process with the student, parent, and administrator, but it may take committed higher education professionals to ignite this process.

So I invite you as a dedicated professional in this field to take note of the aforementioned recommendations to improve the collegiate lives of African-American male undergraduates. It is important to note that these suggestions may not be appropriate for all African-American male students and certainly will not solve every problem. However, with so many students sharing similar experiences as those articulated herein, attempting to apply these recommendations to the African-American male undergraduate population on your campus is certainly worth a try. Accomplishing African-American male student success is certainly not an individual task for professionals. It is just as important for African-American men to accept accountability for their own success as well. With mutually beneficial commitments to advancing African-American male students, positive change is bound to occur and ultimately other conditional college admits, like myself, will become high-achievers and even advance to graduate school and/or a professional career.

References

Bonner II, F. A., *Gifted African American Male College Students: A Phenomenological Study* (Storrs, CT: National Research Center on the Gifted and Talented, 2001).

Bonner II, F. A., "To Be Young, Gifted, African American, and Male," *Gifted Child Today Magazine*, 26(2), Spring 2003, 26–35.

Cuyjet, M. J., *African American men in college* (San Francisco: Jossey-Bass, 2006).

Fries-Britt, S. R., "Identifying and Supporting Gifted African American Men." In Michael Cuyjet (Ed.), *Helping African American Men Succeed in College: New Directions for Student Services*, No. 80 (San Francisco: Jossey-Bass, 1997).

Fries-Britt, S. R., "Moving Beyond Black Achiever Isolation: Experiences of Gifted Black Collegians," *Journal of Higher Education*, 69(5), 1998, 556–576.

Fries-Britt, S. R., "Identity Development of High-Ability Black Collegians." In M. Baxter Magolda (Ed.) *Teaching to Promote Intellectual and Personal Maturity Incorporating Students' Worldviews and Identities into the Learning Process: New Directions in Teaching and Learning*, No. 82 (San Francisco: Jossey-Bass, 2000).

Fries-Britt, S. R., "High Achieving Black Collegians," *About Campus Magazine*, 7(3) (San Francisco: Jossey-Bass, 2002).

Ford, D. Y., Harris III, J. J., Tyson, C. A., and Trotman, M. F., "Beyond Deficit Thinking," *Roeper Review*, 24(2), 2002.

Freeman, K., "No Services Needed?: The Case for Mentoring High-Achieving African American Students," *Peabody Journal of Education*, 74(2), 1999, 15–26.

Guiffrida, D. A., "African-American Student Organizations as Agents of Social Integration," *Journal of College Student Development,* 44(3), 2003, 304–319.

Guiffrida, D. A., "Friends from Home: Assets and Liability to African American Students Attending a Predominantly White Institution," *NASPA Journal,* 41(4), 2004, 693–708.

Harper, S. R., "Enhancing African-American Male Student Outcomes Through Leadership and Active Engagement." In Michael J. Cuyjet (Ed.), *African-American Men in College* (San Francisco: Jossey-Bass, 2006).

Harper, S. R., "Leading the Way: Inside the Experiences of High-Achieving African American Male Students," *About Campus* 10(1), 2004, 8–15.

Hrabowski, III, F. A., Maton, K. I., Greif, G. L. *Beating the Odds: Raising Academically Successful African American Males* (New York, NY: Urban Education, 1998).

LaVant, B. D., Anderson, J. L., and Tiggs, J. W., "Retaining African American Men Through Mentoring Initiatives." In Michael Cuyjet (Ed.), *Helping African-American Men Succeed in College: New Directions for Student Services,* No. 80 (San Francisco: Jossey-Bass, 1997).

Nembhard, J. G., "On the Road to Democratic Economic Participation: Educating African-American Youth in the Postindustrial Global Economy." In Joyce E. King (Ed.), *Black Education: A Transformative Research and Action Agenda for the New Century* (Mahwah, NJ: Lawrence Erlbaum Associates, 2005).

Juliana M. Mosley Anderson

Juliana M. Mosley Anderson serves as the Vice President for Student Affairs at Philander Smith College in Little Rock, Arkansas, and, at the age of 31, she is the youngest member of the President's Cabinet. In this role, Dr. J, as she is known on campus, oversees eight departments that provide academic, social, cultural, and spiritual support to students. Prior to her arrival in Little Rock, Juliana served as the Director of the Office of Multicultural Affairs at John Carroll University in Cleveland, Ohio. Before that, she was the Executive Assistant to the President of Kentucky State University and served as a teaching associate in the Department of Educational Leadership at Miami University.

Dr. J's commitment and service to education and to the community is evident in her honors as a recipient of *Ohio Magazine's* Excellence in Education Awards for 2003 and an inductee to the *Kaleidoscope Magazine* 2004 Forty/Forty Club, which annually recognizes 40 people under the age of forty who have made significant contributions in the Cleveland area. In spring of 2006, Juliana was appointed to a regional board of NASPA and the state board of ACPA, the two largest student affairs associations in the country. Juliana is also a proud member Alpha Kappa Alpha Sorority, Inc.

Juliana received a B.S. degree in Business Education from Ball State University. She then earned an M.A. in Curriculum and Teacher Leadership with concentrated studies in Urban Education, and received a Ph.D. in Educational Leadership from Miami University.

Just Do It—I Did It: Navigating the Doctoral Process

Juliana M. Mosley Anderson

At a time when the average 11-year-old girl was overly concerned about friends, hanging out at the mall, and the newest craze on television, "The Cosby Show," I was thinking about my career and setting lifelong goals. My father gave me a brand new dictionary at the beginning of my sixth grade year, and I christened the inside cover with the following statement, "I will have my Ph.D. by the time I am 28 years old and write mathematics textbooks." I was very fond of math and wanted to become a math teacher, so writing mathematics textbooks just made sense. I still struggle, however, to determine where the desire for a Ph.D. came from. Neither one of my parents is college educated, nor as a child did I know anyone with a Ph.D. In fact, the only doctors I knew were the medical physicians my mother worked with at a local Cleveland hospital. Yet, I was determined to obtain this prestigious degree, of which I knew very little, and began setting incremental goals to ensure my dream's reality.

I thought I would go straight through—high school, bachelors, masters, doctorate—ensuring that I would make my goal by 28 years old. As with every goal, there are some detours along the way; in college I changed my major from math education to business education. Thus, writing mathematics textbooks was no longer on my radar. Then, upon completion of my master's degree, I decided that I needed work experience, so I moved to Houston, Texas, to begin my teaching career. Two short years later, I realized that if any part of my goal stated in that dictionary was going to come to fruition, I needed to go back to school to earn my doctorate. So in the fall of 1998, I called my mentor to seek her advice and guidance regarding the application process. Shortly thereafter, I applied, was accepted, and was on my way back to my alma mater to pursue my doctorate.

Having earned my master's degree from Miami University in May of 1997, I was excited about returning to a place of familiarity and facing a new challenge. I was going back to the same academic department and would essentially have the same professors. The difference was the new academic challenge, for which I was not prepared. While I knew the program would involve more reading, research, and definitely more writing, what I did not anticipate was the political, mental, and emotional aspects interwoven in this academic rite of passage. Also, I was not aware of the departmental changes that had occurred during my two year absence.

Upon entering McGuffey Hall, I expected the Department of Educational Leadership (EDL) to be much like I remembered. I soon found several changes. The leadership of the department had changed significantly. The department chair, the first female and one of the most progressive and liberal leaders in the department's history, had just completed her five year term and was being replaced by a less than transformative male faculty member. Racial diversity, which had been fairly nonrepresentative in the past, had grown exponentially. A faculty that was all white suddenly had a dash of color with not one but two black males being added to the department. The student body also had significantly changed from a handfull of black doctoral candidates to approximately one third of the full-time students being of African descent.

While these changes may seem cosmetic in nature, they were essential to the paradigm shifts that occurred within the department. The combination of less progressive leadership and a major shift in demographics posed some serious challenges regarding curriculum and environment. Although EDL had a tradition of education that was created and suited for middle-class white educators who were seeking a terminal degree to propel their careers, the department had attempted to make diversity a priority. In particular, EDL had published 16 guiding principles, one being diversity, in its commitment to address issues of social justice as its core value to assist the department through its program transformation. Similar to that of the university, increasing racial diversity had been a primary objective of the department. However, when the student body was suddenly infiltrated by changes in race, nationality (several of the students were from the neighboring islands of the Caribbean), culture, and an eclectic array of career backgrounds and goals, the department was not ready to deal with that new reality. The ensuing tension and less than communal behaviors within the department belied the core values it was supposed to espouse, and that ultimately led to our own lived experience with transformational change.

The "Ivory Tower" is often synonymous with the elite and highly educated, implying that persons in academia are members of society's upper echelon. This overly glorified status is a result of systemic structures embedded within society and educational institutions. Thus, those outside the ivory walls who wish to become a member are faced with the challenge of navigating the doctoral process through its maze of politics, discrimination, and various social barriers. I found those barriers almost immediately upon the start of my program, and yet I pushed my way through until the last signature had been obtained on my dissertation.

As a brand new doctoral student, I was assigned a temporary advisor until I had the opportunity to meet other faculty and find a more perfect match. I was initially excited about my temporary advisor because he had been one of my professors from my master's program and served as a reference for me in my doctoral application process. I thought he would make a great advisor during my doctorate, but I soon found that he was not supportive of my goal to complete my doctorate in two years. After all, the average time to complete a doctorate in education is three to four years as a full-time student. The same drive, ambition, and perseverance that existed in the 11-year-old girl was ever present. I would not have expected any less of myself and my capabilities, and at the very least I was willing to give it a try. Despite my strong belief in achieving my goal, I met several people, including my temporary advisor, who told me it was not possible and could not be done. With that kind of negative energy all around me, it is a wonder I did not pack my bags. Instead, it became my fuel to prove them wrong, and more importantly, prove me right. Thus, the task before me was to find an advisor who would be supportive and guide me through this process.

After only a week or two into my program, the department secretary suggested I meet one of the new faculty, Dr. Raymond Terrell, whom she affectionately described as the "black gentleman with gray hair." Upon meeting Dr. Terrell, I was quite anxious and apprehensive about "interviewing" him as a potential advisor and sharing my two-year goal with him, especially since no one else appeared remotely supportive. Nevertheless, I shared my background, research interests, and ambitious degree completion goal. Dr. Terrell not only agreed to be my advisor, but he confirmed that my two year goal was possible and strongly encouraged me with the statement, "Just do it!" In the midst of opposition, God had blessed me with awesome support and guidance through this man, who started as my advisor, became my mentor, and whom I grew to love as a father figure.

With a supportive advisor behind me, I believed I was well on my way to a wonderful educational experience. I soon found, however, that I would be the victim of age, race, gender, and nationality discrimination. In fact, my first reality check occurred during my first class. Like my peers, I, too, had been a teacher, successfully completed a master's degree, and been accepted into the EDL doctoral program. However, there was one thing we did not have in common—age. Most of the students in the program were in their mid-forties or older and were white. There were only three of us under the age of 30, all of whom also happened to be black, with me being the youngster of the group at only 24 years old. One might not see the relevance of age, but it was a huge factor in that I was perceived as not having enough experience, which often led to my peers' discounting my opinions on issues.

During class discussions, my teaching experiences were not given the same credit as those with 15 to 20 years experience as education professionals. I knew that I could not fall prey to the victimization of ageism, so I took advantage of every opportunity to discuss my experiences as a teacher in the inner city schools of Houston, Texas, even equating my two years in that district to the longer careers of my white counterparts' subdued suburban teaching careers. Furthermore, I would remind them that despite my youth, we were in similar places, which meant that the department valued my experience and intellect in the same manner.

While the age discrimination never really ceased, it was certainly overshadowed by the blatant racism or lack of diversity exposure that was occurring in the department. Unlike the ageism that was at the hands of other students, the racism was coming from the faculty and was so institutionally embedded that they seemed to be unaware of their actions. My first encounter with this societal beast came during my second course, a class focusing on women in education. This class was unique from any other course I had encountered at Miami; more than 50 percent of the students were black. During my master's program and in my first doctoral class, there were never more than two of us. Despite this difference, the course started like most classes; the first few moments were spent reviewing the syllabus. I immediately noticed that of the four required books, only one had any mention of a woman of color, Johnetta Cole. The other ten or so women we would study were all white. I found myself in a perplexing situation, as I desperately wanted to voice my distain to the professor but realized the possible political ramifications of doing so.

Upon the advice of my mentor, a faculty member from another department, I addressed the professor about the lack of diversity in the curriculum, recognizing the risk, yet knowing that maintaining the status quo did not benefit anyone. To my amazement, her response was, "Had I known the make-up of the class, I would have selected more blacks." I could not believe what I was hearing, but at the same time I really was not surprised. Her comment indicated that accommodation for diversity in curriculum had to be made only for a racially diverse class of students. Diversity, it seems, could not stand alone as a necessary concept. I went on to inform her that, regardless of the racial make-up of the class, studying a diverse group of women enhanced the course and was necessary to fully appreciate women's contributions to the field of education. I am not sure that she really understood or valued my curricular analysis, so I expanded on this teachable moment in my required class research project, where I chose to focus on the contributions of black women in education. How ironic. I had entered this program to learn and realized there was an opportunity to teach. More importantly, I was beginning to realize the doctoral process was about my growth as I expanded my research and increased my writing and verbal communication. Ultimately I proved that I was worthy of the degree, of earning the title of scholar, and deserving of membership to this very elite group of academicians.

The battle with racism and my scholarly rite of passage appeared to be a reoccurring theme. In one of my research courses, the professor questioned my decision to investigate the racial-identity attitudes of black college students, indicating that blacks have a tendency to research about blacks and that we should broaden our interests. He even strongly suggested that I change my topic. I was infuriated by this comment and narrow-minded philosophy—this program was supposed to be enlightening my intellect, not discouraging my growth. In another conversation with my mentor and Dr. Terrell, I decided to voice my concerns to the professor. In doing so, I asked him if similar comments were made to white students who had the desire to research suburban schools where the populations are mostly white. The professor further implied that the students' experiences existed in these districts, giving validity to their interests. While I am sure it was not intended, his argument supported my research interest as well. Thus, I proceeded with my project, and at the end of the course he stated that it was one of the best research projects he had read in his 25 years of teaching.

There were several other discriminatory acts that I and other students of color experienced, but instead of belaboring these instances I chose to refocus on the underlying elements. Due to the negative experiences students had encountered and as a result of numerous complaints, the department realized that some course of positive action was needed in order to address the racial divide that threatened to destroy the program. Thus, under the leadership of Dr. Terrell and a few student leaders who were willing to battle the internal politics, a process to evaluate the racial, community, and curricular issues was begun in the EDL. While the initial objective may have been to discuss issues that all students were having regarding the Department of Educational Leadership, we solely discussed concerns related to black students. After all, only black students were invited to attend the meeting. Specifically, the meeting consisted of three faculty and three student representatives, which led to the formation of a committee charged to further explore the issues and make suggestions to the department chair.

Unfortunately the entire process, spanning several months and numerous meetings with an outside consultant and the internal investigative committee, taught me nothing and only reinforced my values and beliefs. A process that was initiated to deal with issues of black students (racial in nature) turned into an all-inclusive community building process. While this broader objective may have been needed, it took away from the initial concerns of race relations. In my experience this happens all the time—we start off trying to combat racial issues and that turns into a multicultural process, where every issue is considered and combated all at once. Yes, these other concerns should be addressed, but we need to deal with the initial issue first. Since the committee had determined there were racial matters, then those should have taken first priority. Once we had effectively dealt with those concerns, reaching a level of comfort by those affected, we could then have moved on to other issues. As usual, society and even its educational institutions that are responsible for teaching and leading continue to remain stagnant in their quest to combat racial issues, which prohibits the growth of society. I believe that race is the most prominent barrier among Americans. Gender and class are also factors, but most of the problems in this country stem from race. This should have been the focus of our dialogue and activities, not community building. Deal with the racial issues and community will come.

Perhaps I really did not expect any major change to occur in regards to the initial problems. There have been racial problems in this country since European immigration began, and there have been no solutions. So, why did the EDL believe it was capable of eliminating its racial problems in eight months? If it were that easy, people would not continuously have to fight for equality, acceptance, and respect. Unfortunately, I feel that the racial attitudes I endured during my tenure at Miami are a common phenomenon for other black or doctoral students of color at other institutions, and these attitudes will continue in future generations because critical transformation has yet to occur. I honestly believe that others will share my story because no community can be built when the racial barriers have not been torn down first.

In my reflection on those two years of my life, I think about the critical elements to my success. Yes, by the grace of God I became the first black student in the EDL to complete all requirements for the doctorate in just two years, 23 months to be exact (one year before me, a white female also completed her program in two years). As opposed to Doctor of Philosophy, a Ph.D. should be interpreted as a Doctor of Politics. Obtaining this degree had very little to do with intellectual growth; navigating the political waters was definitely the pinnacle of this process. Even with ageism, racism, and gender discrimination ever present, I knew that my faith, persistence, and support from others would carry me through. In all that I do, I give credit to my Heavenly Father who guides and protects me, for which I am eternally grateful. I am also thankful for the earthly people He has placed in my life who offer wisdom and comfort. My support system is phenomenal, and they were on the battlefield during those critical two years. While all of my support (husband, parents, friends, and mentors) helped me to succeed with their encouraging words, listening ears, and constant prayers, there was one who made the ultimate difference, Dr. Raymond Terrell. When I wanted to quit, he encouraged me to keep going and said, "Just do it!" When racism kept rearing its ugly head, he gave me comfort and said, "Just do it!" When people discouraged me from completing my degree in record time, he said, "Just do it!" So, "I did it," completing the degree and affirming my declaration in my sixth grade dictionary. Not only had I obtained my Ph.D. by the time I was 28, I finished two years early, at the age of 26. With one goal successfully met, the next is yet to come. The inside front cover of my dissertation states that I will be a college president by the time I am 40. I pray that I will write another story honoring the fruition of that dream also.

Part 3

Teaching and Learning, Challenge and Support

Culture Shock in the Heartland Be Stoney

Giving All, Getting Half Jean Moule

Be Stoney

Dr. Be Stoney is currently an associate professor in the Department of Secondary Education at Kansas State University where she teaches Multicultural Education and Diversity courses. She received a B.S. degree in Special Education and Health and a M.Ed. in Kinesiology both from the University of Texas at El Paso. She received her Ph.D. in General Special Education and Multicultural Education from the University of Texas at Austin.

For the last 18 years, Dr. Stoney has served as a trainer and consultant in the areas of Special Education and Multicultural Education in public schools and in higher education. She also serves as the Midwest Equity Assistance Center Race Relation and Technical Consultant, conducting equity workshops and diversity training for public schools in Iowa, Kansas, Missouri, and Nebraska.

On the Kansas State University campus, she serves as the chair for Black Faculty/Staff Alliance (BFSA), serves as a member on the Developing Scholars Committee, Diversity Advisory Council, the University General Education Council, the College of Education Academic Review Committee, and McNair Mentor.

When Dr. Stoney is not busy serving on committees, she officiates women's basketball at all levels and serves as a Big XII Official Evaluator.

Her major research interests are in the areas of diversity, multiculturalism, and recruitment and retention of students of color in predominantly white institutions.

Culture Shock in the Heartland: Surviving on a Predominantly White Campus as an African-American Female Professor

Be Stoney, Ph.D.

I have known from an early age that I always wanted to be a college professor, but I was not sure in which field I would study. I am from a long line of educators, a third generation teacher. I am number six of eight children, and six of us have earned college degrees. Although I am second generation masters of education, I am the first generation of Ph.D. The bar was set high at an early age for me, and I have responded to many challenges that have prepared me for what I encounter at my institution.

As an African-American female professor on a predominantly white campus, there are three major challenges that, when taken together, form what I call culture shock. The first challenge is adapting to my white environment. Second is the challenge of adjusting to the small number of tenured-track African-American professors on campus who are willing to serve as mentors. The third, and most difficult challenge, is the silent climate issues. It took a friend to explain the silent strategies of how to survive on a predominantly white campus. While learning how to adapt and survive to my new life in the heartland, it took four years to be accepted in an environment that I define as unfriendly, hostile, and lonely. I chronicle my voice, my story, based on my experiences and how these experiences were shocking and many times traumatic.

Adapting to My Environment

Adapting to the culture of my new surroundings and surviving in my environment took four grueling years. My most challenging experience was to understand who I am as an African-American female professor in this white and often hostile environment. I tried to make friends, but to no avail; it was difficult. I was not sure whether I was too friendly or too outspoken for my new Midwestern peers. I did learn quickly that my new colleagues were not ready for an outspoken, confident, African-American woman who made them feel uncomfortable and frightened. They thought I posed a threat to them. Once my peers learned about me and understood who I am as a person, I did not appear as a threat any longer. I believe what frightened my peers were my confident approach and my work ethics, as well as my relationships with people. A peer once told me, "You do not carry yourself like a junior faculty member. You appear to be a seasoned faculty member." My peer went on to say, "Most African-American junior faculty members do not know much about higher education and need more guidance than white junior faculty members." Enraged by his comment and his silent backhanded compliment, I wondered at that moment, why I was here. Will I have to deal with this type of mentality daily? This was my introduction to understanding where I "fit" into the "order" of my college as an African-American faculty member. According to my peer, I fit somewhere between a novice instructor and a first year graduate student. Unbeknownst to my peer, I had five years of teaching experiences in higher education; however, I did not feel as though I needed to disclose this information to validate my credibility.

Understanding my white surroundings in the classroom with students was another culture shock I faced with great difficulty. As an urban person, moving to the rural Midwest engendered some culture shock, but teaching classes with only white students was an even greater culture shock. My prior experience with students had always been in diverse settings. The current configuration was a new experience for me. I had taught multicultural education and diversity courses to in-service teachers, adults who are employed in different working industries, and undergraduate students. The course discussions focused on issues relating to learning styles of children of color; understanding culture and how culture is important to students of color; and how to relate and work with parents from different racial/ethnic identities, race, gender, social economic status, and sexual orientation. I learned the hard way that most white students are not ready to discuss hard issues because they are not ready to face both past and present relationships between African Americans and whites. As an African-American female professor teaching about racism, prejudices, and biases, the white students clearly expressed that I was harsh toward white people, I did not like whites, and I needed to learn to be more sensitive, especially toward white males.

I believe my teaching methods are not biased against white students, but I want white students to gain awareness in the notions of privileges, earned and unearned, of white supremacy, and how people learn their biases toward others who often do not look like them. Most of my students found it difficult to adjust to our conversations because they felt uncomfortable, experienced or attested to "white guilt," or wanted to apologize for their race. I asked my students, "Why did you sign up for my class?" Most students responded, "I thought the course would be interesting," "You are the first African-American professor I have taken a class with," or my personal favorite, "I thought you were white. That is why I enrolled in the class."

Understanding my white surroundings in the classroom was not only challenging but often different each time class met. For example, frequently students would challenge my expertise or would want to verify the information by asking a white colleague. During a discussion, one student openly stated, "I asked my advisor to clear up this issue regarding African-American children and special education. According to my advisor, African-American children are not over represented in special education and that your information is incorrect." Hanging my head in disbelief, I asked this student, "What is your advisor's research agenda and what knowledge, if any, does he have about the over-representation of African-American children in special education?" The room was silent as was the student. I asked, "When a white colleague is lecturing, do you question or challenge his or her knowledge at the same level in which you question me? Do you think that I am not competent in my field?" Regardless of how many researchers I refer to, citations I use, or references I disseminate, my knowledge is always challenged.

Regarding my white surroundings and the culture of my surroundings, I have learned how to survive in the hostile classroom based on three strategies. First, as students challenge my knowledge, I challenge what they have learned in class. We discuss what they thought they knew, which was very little. We then talk about what they would like to know and how much information they have retained throughout the semester. Finally, we discuss what they have learned about others who are different from them, but more importantly, how much they have grown personally.

Second, when students think that I am biased toward African Americans, I ask, "Am I not biased towards whites?" I teach my classes focusing on all racial/ethnic groups, not only African Americans. It amazes me how little white students know about their culture.

Third, when students are uncomfortable with our class discussions, I challenge them to look inside themselves and ask "Why?" Why do you feel uncomfortable? What that you have learned in your early stages of life about others who are different does not hold true to what you are being taught. I am fascinated with the idea that most of my white students are often hesitant to verbalize the racial identities of African Americans. The word is often mumbled or they are afraid to use the word black for fear of offending someone. Finally, it takes 15 weeks (one semester) to get white students to understand that we live in two different worlds of consciousnesses on our campus—a world that is designed for white people and a world that is designed for people of color. I live in the latter and have learned to adapt to the former on my campus.

Who Are the Mentors on This Campus?

Knowing and understanding my white surroundings, another challenge I had to conquer was Where are the African-American mentors on this campus? On predominantly white campuses across America, African-American professors find it difficult to find mentors who are willing to guide them through the tenure process and the process of adapting to the culture of the campus. Although I was assigned a mentor during my first year, there was little interaction and guidance. I felt I was not receiving the same type of guidance I observed other white junior faculty members were given. For example, my junior faculty peers were co-presenting at major conferences with their mentors, or they were asked to serve as co-principal investigators on grants. I was never asked to do either. Yet, as grants were being written, I was asked for my vitae so that my name could be added as the multicultural component. However, I never participated in the implementation of those grants. I felt I was being pushed aside when I asked, "If you are to use my vitae, why can I not be a part of the implementation of the grants?" Strange, I never received an honest response. I was told, "You do not have to worry about participating in the implementation because you have enough to deal with regarding your teaching load and preparing for tenure in the future." I was angry because I could not get a straight answer from my mentor; therefore, I sought advice outside my college to gain a better understanding of how this process works. Needless to say, I received the same response. I learned later that their use of my name without my input was not the correct process. My vitae had been used to meet their criteria for the grant by showing that someone of color was written into the grant.

In my second year, I was assigned a different mentor and even less mentoring occurred. By this time, I had lost two valuable years for research and scholarly work. When I asked my mentor to review my writings, he felt that I was incapable of producing scholarly writing. I solicited another colleague (a white female) to read my work and she stated, "You should focus more on researching white students instead of African Americans. Tenured faculty members tend to think this is not scholarly work nor a good research agenda." The wind left my sails. I felt like I was treading in shark-infested waters with little to no chance of making it to shore alive. I was at the end of my rope and my confidence was sinking quickly.

Where are the mentors who are willing to assist me in being a successful African-American female professor as they have successfully mentored my white peers? In my third year, I, along with other seasoned survivors of this mentoring system, were kicked out of the nest to make room for the arrival of new junior faculty members. Even though some seasoned survivors remained with their mentors, I was left alone to work independently, checking in occasionally with my former mentor. I was like a fish out of water, not knowing when I would breathe my last breath of air or how I was to maintain what little air I had to survive.

It took four years to finally connect with a mentor whose main interest was helping me succeed in my career. My mentor has guided me through the pitfalls of destruction and the impossible barriers to climb, to reach tangible goals of success. In just one year, I was able to write five manuscripts for publication and to produce a book chapter. My mentor was an African-American man. The relationship I established with my colleague and mentor was unlike any professional development I had experienced with my white mentors. My mentor reignited my passion for teaching, inspired my passion for writing, and refueled my passion to believe in myself. My mentor and colleague provided positive suggestions and feedback regarding my writing. We met weekly to find out how I was coping and, more importantly, he restored my inner strength that I had lost as an African-American female professor. I appreciate my mentor and colleague because he taught me how to weather the storms of destruction, recognize the pitfalls in conversations, and avoid wolves dressed in sheep's clothing.

Climate Issues

I also learned how climate issues could disrupt my progress as an African-American female professor. The climate issues I faced were lack of trust, loneliness, questions about my membership as a professor, and others wanting to see me as damaged goods. Damaged goods are like a can with a tattered and torn label that no one will select unconsciously. The can has dents and tears due to improper handling. It is unattractive and unappealing. People unconsciously push the can aside to reach for a can that has an appealing label. At the end of the day, the tattered and torn labeled can still remains on the shelf alone. The lack of trust and loneliness were two areas I found difficult to separate. I did not know whom to trust; who would not treat me as though it were all in my imagination how people were treating me. This led to my loneliness. Once a colleague asked if I were intending to sit at a front table for a presentation we were attending? My response was yes. His comment was, "The back is reserved for blacks." Without missing a beat, I commented, "You did not receive the memo that the front is reserved for blacks and the back is reserved for PWT like you." Unfamiliar with the acronym, I explained the meaning to him, and he was embarrassed. He later apologized, but the impact for me was already felt. How could he bring himself to make this comment to me and assume it was acceptable? What made matters worse was that our presenter was an African-American female.

I believe my membership in the university environment was questioned because I felt like the outsider. As a multiculturalist and diversity trainer, my discipline crosses every discipline in the college, yet few requested my expertise. It took four years before a peer asked me about multicultural or special education issues regarding students of color. Four years. Does it take that long to establish a working relationship with your colleagues?

The tendency of others to see me as damaged goods was the toughest climate issue for me at my institution. This was a "set me up for failure" connection in my college. For example, I was asked by the associate dean to chair our NCATE (National Council for Accreditation of Teacher Education) Standard 4 on Diversity committee. The NCATE Standard 4 on Diversity are standards that accredited schools, colleges, and departments of education use to prepare teachers and other professional personnel for work in elementary and secondary schools. Instead of selecting a tenured professor, I, a junior faculty, was assigned this position. My job was to compile information, collect syllabi from all disciplines, and discuss how diversity was incorporated into the curriculum of the disciplines. I had to write an extensive report and turn this information in to a larger committee. When the information was finalized for print, I did not have the opportunity to review the report, nor was I a part of the editing and final process. The final report submitted was not the original report. The report had been rewritten.

My leadership in generating the report was somewhat recognized, but not my dedication, contribution, nor the months I spent working diligently on the project. I questioned why a junior faculty member was selected to chair this committee and not a full professor. Chairing this committee caused me to lose one year of my writing time and a good piece of my sanity. When I discussed this matter with the dean, he replied, "Your department chair should have spoken on your behalf." How do you respond to this statement when the dean and your department chair are close personal friends? As a junior faculty, how do you say no to a request from the associate dean of curriculum without having this penalty held over your head before tenure? Response: you will be perceived as damaged goods. I endured that year as I did the other years. Even though the leader of my college or institution could change the climate in which I operated, I learned to operate in the climate based on the changes I needed for survival.

Summing It Up

Personally, I have learned to recover, adjust, adapt, and understand my role and contributions to my college and institution as an African-American female professor. I found advocates whose beliefs in my contributions to our institution are nonjudgmental. I realized that, once I found advocates who understood my position as an African American, a woman, a multiculturalist, and a professor, I changed how I survived on a predominantly white campus.

I have had discussions with my dean regarding the college climate, my personality, and my attitude. I have learned that I am well respected and liked by all my peers and they do want to see me succeed. I did not realize most of my colleagues felt this way. Although he could not change the climate issues discussed, the dean worked on changing the college's mentoring program for faculty members. I was reinstated into the mentoring program and have achieved success on many levels.

As for my white environment, surviving was only the beginning. Learning how to decode the silent messages from white colleagues and students and dealing with them were challenges I mastered. My mentor will always be regarded as my foundation, the person who gave me strength and taught me how to persevere. The climate issues are slow to change, but I have changed the climate to adapt to me, not me to adapt to the climate. White students will continue to enroll in my classes, and I welcome them to challenge my expertise as I challenge their knowledge. Surviving on predominantly white college campuses is no longer a challenge for African-American professors but a rite of passage for success.

Jean Moule

Dr. Jean Moule was born in South Carolina and raised in New York City and Los Angeles. She earned her B.A. from the University of California at Berkeley, where she studied art, psychology and education, and was arrested in the Free Speech Movement.

While she and her husband raised three children she earned a M.S. from the University of Oregon and a Ph.D. from Oregon State University. She is a tenured faculty member at OSU, where she teaches multicultural issues in education for K-12 pre-service teachers. She initiated and continues to coordinate the Immersion Professional Teacher Education Program, which places OSU student teachers in culturally and linguistically diverse schools in Portland and Salem, Oregon's two largest metropolitan areas.

Through her experiences as a student and a teacher, Dr. Moule has come to understand how students are harmed by the racism formerly institutionalized in Oregon's laws and still embedded in many hearts. She co-authored the text *Cultural Competence, A Primer for Educators*, filled with many stories of schooling and some from her own family. She hopes that her work will help Oregon and the nation's children, including her six grandchildren, to have culturally competent teachers.

To balance her stressful professional life, Dr. Moule joins ski patrol in the winter and participates in masters track and field in the summer.

Giving All, Getting Half

Jean Moule, Ph.D.

Preparing students to teach in diverse settings highlights the overwhelming presence of whiteness in education (Sleeter, 2001). My college and my colleagues have made efforts to recruit a more racially diverse student population into our teacher education programs, yet the majority of our preservice teachers are white. Our faculty is also overwhelmingly white. I am one of only 10 African Americans in the university's 1,200 tenured or tenure-track faculty and the only visible person of color on our teacher education faculty. Still, we focus on social justice in our programs and work to prepare all of our students for culturally and linguistically diverse classrooms.

For me, when the word racial is added to social justice, the stakes are raised and the need for action by groups or individuals of color may be heightened. "The strategy of those who fight for racial social justice is to unmask and expose racism in all of its various permutations" (Ladson-Billings, 2000, p. 264). As someone committed to racial social justice, I am compelled to do this unmasking.

This story details some of my struggles as I have tried to walk the balance between activism and "getting along" in our teacher education program. While my white colleagues could work toward social justice by acknowledging and challenging socially acceptable notions of racism, such as declaring a strong stand against overt racism, my imperative was more extensive. Thomas (2001) saw the same choicelessness widely reflected in the women she studied, "African-American women and Latina scholars see a personal mission of social change as a fundamental part of their professional responsibilities" (p. 82). My colleagues belong to mainstream white American culture and cannot deeply understand being a person of color in our society. They may neither recognize, nor have the same need to fight, more subtle racism.

Some of the ways in which I worked to combat racism in all its forms increased my workload. For instance, I NEEDED to recruit students of color for our program from outside the regular channels and process, and I was COMPELLED to develop new courses based on our efforts to implement a social justice perspective. I sensed the need to "reach out of the box" to make a difference, rather than simply acknowledge the need for change and add on a "color coat" at a superficial level (Moule, 2004).

Eventually I undertook a five-year study of my work, and my analysis of the data indicates that my self-initiated activity as an isolated individual of color working toward social justice was the most prevalent reason for my overload (Moule, 2005). In that study I shared my results organized by my educator/scholar's role: teaching, advising, research, and university service. I concluded with a discussion of our struggles at different levels of racial identity and interaction.

As a result, this additional work that I MUST do impacted my publication record and the outcome of my journey to promotion and tenure at our university. The off-campus and out-of-the-office activities and the difficulty of managing my workload, as well as the controversy around my activism, jeopardized my future as a tenured professor and also contributed to significant emotional and physical difficulties. I am pleased that in this forum I can be more open. Here I am able to share the emotional and physical cost of giving all, and getting half, as I was tenured but not promoted.

As I struggled to maintain my self-respect and integrity after a not-so-nice, not-so-successful battle for promotion and tenure, the following email from an acquaintance on campus became a minor link in the chain that helps me stay where I am not always appreciated:

> Those I know who have been tenured without being promoted are people I respect tremendously... the impact they've made and continue to make for students and for the overall university community is crucial to our collective future, and—unfortunately—is often outside what is recognized by the promotion and tenure system. I don't know anything about the factors in your situation, but I certainly see you as someone who makes that kind of difference here. You've devoted yourself to doing work about which you are passionate, in the way you know it needs to be done. I see that as living and working with integrity... but I sure don't think you're obliged to feel happy about getting only half of what you asked for! (email, name withheld [used with permission], May 18, 2005)

The battle has been long and hard. I am exhausted. My bulletin board is covered with quotes that speak continually of advancing against the odds. My favorites today are: "The road is very long, the challenges are multiple, the pain is unavoidable, the depth of our love is fathomless, and the degree of our effort must increase as day follows day" (from a student, Lua Siegel, 2001) and "I have allies, I have a strong family, and I have my faith in God. I will continue as long as I can" (Jean Moule).

A few years ago, in an effort to explore my role at my university with others I wrote the following metaphor:

> It is as if we are all on a river that flows quietly and gently along. Most of my friends, students, and colleagues float on this river in a strong, sturdy boat of their majority status—a boat I cannot get into because I am not white. The river, our societal mainstream, is accepted and hardly noticed. I manage to swim or float alongside the boat as I am learning how to navigate this mainstream. Every once in a while someone in the boat notices my struggle and tosses

out an inner tube or briefly holds my hand. And then sometimes, someone reaches out and pushes my head under with, "Just get over this race thing, Jean." I sputter, resurface and continue on. In the long run, I figure it makes sense to construct a raft for myself. So while I talk to those in the boat and we run difficult rapids together, at the same time I must lash together whatever supportive materials I can find. The response? "Hey, how come Jean gets a raft?" When I say, "Because I can't get in the boat with you and I'm getting tired of staying afloat without more support," some say, "What boat?" (Moule, 2003, p. 3 [adapted from Journal entry 11/19/01])

While many grapple with the complex issues raised by this metaphor, its toll on those of us who struggle in the water is both stressful and, in its extreme, career and life-threatening. My own health struggles in the last four years have ranged from high blood pressure to unexplained chronic pain to migraines and a lowered immune system. While I entered the academy with reserves of physical energy (I ran a marathon shortly before I entered higher education) and emotional reserves (my husband and I had just finished raising three children to advanced degrees and celebrated our 30th happy wedding anniversary), I am now finding it physically difficult to rise refreshed, mentally difficult to engage each new problem to solve, and emotionally difficult to find hope where once I saw intriguing challenges.

My journey is not dissimilar from those of many other faculty of color (see Turner and Myers, 2000). Recruited due to both excellence and ethnicity, I came into higher education and multicultural education from a career as an elementary teacher and an expert in the field of talented and gifted education. As I began my doctoral studies, I encountered the need for diverse teachers at all levels. I decided that I could fulfill that role at the university and that my presence might help us increase the percentage of students of color in our graduate programs, which it has. My 2005 textbook, with co-author Jerry Diller, *Cultural Competence: A Primer for Educators* is well-respected in the state and is used in many college and university courses across the nation. My on-campus, Multicultural Issues in Education, course is popular, my section filling before others. The unique immersion program I began has been recognized at college, university, and state levels as an innovative and effective way to prepare preservice teachers to work with culturally and linguistically diverse K-8 students. Finally, over 50 percent of the African-American students in our graduate education programs are there as a direct result of my recruitment efforts over the last seven years.

Aspects of these efforts were often met by resistance from my colleagues. Recruiting and program development that took me off campus were seen as shirking my duty to be physically available for drop-in appointments with colleagues and advisees. My record of attendance at scheduled faculty meetings was high (in addition, I sometimes connected by phone while at conferences), yet I was not as available for spur-of-the-moment work or meetings. My sense is that some folks' unconscious expectation that I should be at their beck and call, and be there to represent the faculty of color viewpoint, caused them to hold me to a higher standard. It seemed as if my absences were more noted and deemed more grievous than others' absences.

Collins (1990) explains the need to situate one's struggle as part of the larger picture, and she emphasizes visualizing that such struggles will make a difference:

> The interplay between black women's oppression and black women's activism...views the world as a dynamic place where the goal is not merely to survive or to fit in or to cope; rather.... there is always choice, and the power to act, no matter how bleak the situation may appear to be. Viewing the world as one in the making raises the issue of individual responsibility for bringing about change. (p. 237)

During the time I worked to make inroads into our campus racism, I have become aware of the invisible burden that faculty of color carry into their teaching and learning situations that may not be recognized by others, or sometimes, by themselves. Not only does this burden color my conversations, decisions, and interactions, but its usually hidden nature makes it more difficult to complete my professional responsibilities.

While we may try to alleviate and mitigate many aspects of this burden, it is not possible to remove them. In spring 2001, with input from two other African-American faculty at our university, I developed this list of possible burdens on faculty of color. In the second column, I will note how I work to lighten the burden.

100   Jean Moule

Burden	Lightening the Load
1 People on campus are surprised to see me, based on my color.	Park close to building, limit walks on campus (make office an oasis), go with a colleague for distraction, go to the same places where I am already known, self-talk before walking on campus.
2 Occasionally there is an overtly racist act in my presence that surprises and disturbs me. (Did I really see/hear that? Yes, I did!)	Ignore as possible, but process. Sometimes confront.
3 Reacting to verbal and non-verbal responses to my presence on campus is a level of mental and emotional work that most of my colleagues do not share.	Reduce level of mental and emotional work by limiting exposure.
4 People are more likely to exhibit prejudice from unconscious rather than conscious bias, and may not recognize when this is happening. However, the fact that this bias exists IS often in my consciousness and therefore a level of mental and emotional work that most of my colleagues and I do not share.	Act as if it is not there, assume the best. In some situations, it is possible to make unconscious biases conscious.
5 Oregon has a particularly racist past. My race and my reading of Oregon history have made me more consciously aware of this than my colleagues and students. I am more likely to see and be reminded of the current consequences of past racism. For example, while reading a student's statement, "there was little diversity in my community," I am very aware that the person who made the statement is probably totally ignorant of why this	Recognize that students' and others' perspectives may simply be a factor of their upbringing. Forgive ignorance.

Giving All, Getting Half

phenomenon occurs in Oregon, e.g., exclusion laws, early and wide-spread KKK, numerous sundown towns. Every time I read such statements, I am reminded of the history that produced this student's monocultural upbringing.

6. Some of my students question my competency based on their overt or covert racism. This raises the standard I must hold in my teaching.

   Continue to do my best.

7. Having faced dead ends because of race or gender in the past, I am more likely to fear such in the future, so I tend to rely on my own resources when possible.

   Try to trust and collaborate.

8. I am asked to teach or speak in some areas and am assumed to have specialized knowledge based solely on my race.

   Consider each request and respond appropriately if I actually possess the knowledge and perspective needed.

9. My adaptations to these differences and multiple realities include my understanding of these differences and realities and the fact that others may not understand. This causes me to be divided in my perspective taking as I recognize both viewpoints. This may result in my participating in my own oppression through acknowledging and inadvertently accepting the other perspective.

   Try to maintain own perspective and not add to my oppression.

10. I am surrounded by people who do not share my racial burden (the items in this list).

    Network at conferences. Become involved with integrated school staffs in distant locations so that I am in contact with people who do share my racial perspective, and/or work in diverse settings.

11 I have to decide whether to reveal the race-based nature of some of my actions and decisions (such as constructing this list). That may add to the burden of race and may cause increased distance.	Do it when expedient and necessary. Pick and chose battles so that I might live to "fight" another day.
12 My colleagues reading this list may be tempted to say "move on," or come up with an oppression they experience occasionally and say it is the same.	Forgive, understand.

This list was an early attempt to inform my colleagues about the difference that race makes. I continue to expand this part of my research (see Moule and Waldschmidt, 2003, Moule, 2004, and Moule, 2005). Making this list and writing this story have helped me to see myself better. As attributed to Maya Angelou, "Society's view of the black woman is such a threat to her well-being that she will die daily unless she determines how she sees herself." I may persevere for a while longer while understanding that the struggle I feel "living this way... with the daily indignities... with a broken heart" (Nile and Straton, 2003, p. 5) is not particularly emotionally or physically healthy.

Returning to the river metaphor, I do find some professional hope for the future: "The challenge for those in the water and for those in the boat is to reach out for each other on our common journey while aiming to make a difference in the very river that carries us all along" (Moule, 2003, p. 3). I keep a file of evidence of the small changes I see in my field and among my colleagues that are adding up to a different outcome for students and faculty of color at all levels.

My latest personal challenge is: How do I not let my current state of cynicism and decreasing hope from the outcome of my promotion and tenure review infect others? I have to decide daily to carry on against the odds, take up a shield of faith, and recognize that this IS a battle. My best hope for the future is to keep fighting on whatever ground is under my feet and mine to defend and expand. Finally, I find well-being and renewed strength in my life verse that uses a different river metaphor:

"She shall be like a tree planted by the rivers of water that brings forth her fruit in its season... and whatsoever she does shall prosper" (Psalm 1).

References

Collins, P. H., *Black Feminist Thought: Knowledge, Consciousness, and the Politics of Empowerment* (Boston: Unwin Hyman, 1990).

Diller, J. V. and Moule, J., *Cultural Competence: A Primer for Educators* (Cincinnati, OH: Wadsworth, 2005).

Ladson-Billings, G., "Racialized Discourses and Ethnic Epistemologies." In N. K. Denzin and Y. S. Lincoln (Eds.), *Handbook of Qualitative Research*, 2e (Thousand Oaks, CA: Sage, 2000), 257–277.

Moule, J., "Implementing a Social Justice Perspective in Teacher Education: Invisible Burden for Faculty of Color" *Teacher Education Quarterly*, 32(4) 2005, 23–42.

Moule, J., "Safe and Growing Out of the Box: Immersion for Social Change." In J. J. Romo, P. Bradfield and R. Serrano (Eds.), *Reclaiming Democracy: Multicultural Educators' Journeys Toward Transformative Teaching* (Upper Saddle River, NJ: Pearson Merrill, 2004), 147-171.

Moule, J., "Aiming to Make a Difference" (Corvallis, OR: Commencement address for graduate students, 2003), accessed February 7, 2005, *http://oregonstate.edu/education/news/caddress.html*.

Moule, J. and Waldschmidt, E. D., "Face-to-Face over Race: Personal Challenges from Instituting a Social Justice Perspective in our Teacher Education Program" *Teacher Education and Practice*, 16(2), 2003, 121-142.

Nile, L. N. and Straton, J. C., "Beyond Guilt: How to Deal with Societal Racism" *Multicultural Education*, Summer 2003, 2-6.

Sleeter, C. E., "Preparing Teachers for Culturally Diverse Schools: Research and the Overwhelming Presence of Whiteness" *Journal of Teacher Education*, 52(2), 2001, 94-106.

Thomas, G. D., "The Dual Role of Scholar and Social Change Agent: Reflections from Tenured African American and

Latina Faculty." In R. O. Mabokela and A. L. Green (Eds.), *Sisters of the Academy: Emergent Black Women Scholars in Higher Education* (Sterling, VA: Stylus, 2001), 80-91.

Turner, C. S. V. and Myers, S. L., Jr., *Faculty of Color in Academe: Bittersweet Success* (Needham Heights, MA: Allyn & Bacon, 2000).

Part 4

Outsiders within Our Organizations

Reflections on a Decade of Great Expectations — Joyce Simons

1 Day and 3 Hours — Nell Lewis

Alone and Assailed in the Heartland of America — Stephen K. Appiah-Padi

Know Your Place or No You May Not — Pam Mitchell-Crump

Joyce Simons

Dr. Joyce Simons has been in the field of education for over three decades. She currently serves as Dean of the Division of Academic Support Services of Nyack College in New York. This division includes the Department of First Year Studies, Higher Education Opportunity Program, Nyack's Introduction to Academia program, Academic Success Center, Writing Center, Disabilities Support Services, and the ESL program. Dr. Simons is an appointed professor in the School of Education at Nyack. Prior to coming to Nyack, Dr. Simons worked as an assistant professor at the Borough of Manhattan Community College and as an instructor at Hostos Community College, both in New York.

Dr. Simons was born in New York City where she attended elementary and high school. She holds a bachelor of science degree in Human Development and Family Studies from Cornell University. Additionally, she has a master's degree in Educational Administration, a master's degree in Reading Education, and a Doctorate in Curriculum and Teaching, all from Columbia University Teachers College.

Dr. Simons firmly believes that teachers, administrators, and parents must work collaboratively to assist young people in bridging the gap between "ability and productivity." To this end, she founded Positive Interventions, Inc. in 1996 which is an educational consultant firm specializing in providing professional staff development workshops for teachers, administrators, and parents. These workshops have been presented at MIT, the Einstein Enrichment Program at the Albert Einstein School of Medicine, and Columbia University to name a few.

Dr. Simons serves as a board member for several community organizations and professional organizations.

Reflections on a Decade of Great Expectations

Joyce Simons

"The level of disappointment that one experiences in any given situation is directly proportionate to the distance between one's expectations going into that situation and the reality of what actually exists." (Quote from Dr. A.R. Bernard)

For the past decade, I have had the privilege of working at an institution whose main campus is located 20 miles north of New York City. It is an evangelical Christian institution where faculty and students proclaim Jesus Christ as Lord and Savior of their lives. The college of 2004 is a vastly different institution from the one I entered in 1995. It is now, by far, one of the most ethnically diverse colleges within the Council for Christian Colleges and Universities (CCCU), ranking number 2 out of 105 for African-American enrollments (U.S. Department of Education, 2002). In the entering class of 2003, 27 percent of the students were African American in contrast to 12 percent in 1995. In 2003, 14 percent of the full-time instructional faculty was African American as opposed to 3 percent in 1995. However promising these figures appear, the institution continues to struggle with effective ways to integrate and deal with students, faculty, and administrators of color. Ten years ago, as an idealistic educator and administrator, I expected the "Christian" institution to have transcended racial, gender, and cultural differences. Today, I realize that the commonality of a Christian faith is not enough to transcend these human limitations. In order to remain effective as a leader, I have had to readjust my expectations of this Christian institution and develop coping mechanisms to remain effective and to survive as a leader.

I have found myself in a variety of situations throughout my years on university campuses. This Christian institution presented me with a set of unique situations. I have developed questions about conflict between how blacks and whites worship and about the passive approach to recruiting individuals of color (two aspects of my work in particular are of great concern to me.) Differences in worship styles may be considered a minor area by some, but it is one that has a tremendous impact on students of color. Denominational differences in worship styles were quite an issue when I arrived on campus in 1995. The spirited worship of many of the students of color presented a challenge for many who preferred a quieter tone of worship. The faculty in 1995 was overwhelmingly white, while the faces of the student population presented a different picture. As the population became more diverse, I found myself advocating for the many students of color on campus. Despite the resistance, more acceptance of the diverse worship styles of all the students is beginning to occur.

Another area in which I have had to play an active role has been in the implementation of the college's diversity agenda. Rather than waiting for "people" to find qualified individuals of color, I have realized that I had to actively work with the institution to "find" more minorities. Although faculty diversity has been a goal of the institution, its approaches to recruitment have not always been aggressive. When openings occurred in the 1990s, department heads seemed unable to find faculty of color. Often I would hear comments like, "A black person with a Ph.D. has so many options; why would they want to come here?" If they did receive a résumé, it was often scrutinized for what it did not contain. A few years after I had been at the college, I was asked to submit a list of professional publications that black faculty would most likely look to when seeking a position in higher education. Although I submitted the names of several professional journals, I was quite disappointed because I rarely saw advertisements for positions at our college. Here again, I was forced to readjust my expectation that they would do something, and I crafted a plan of my own that would work toward a solution to the problem. I began by hiring people within my own department. I am happy to say that a number of those whom I hired went on to fill other key positions within the college. Subsequently, over the past three years, both the president and provost of the college have made hiring faculty of color a high priority. I have been instrumental in bringing many qualified African Americans to the college.

Staying Connected

Advocacy for my students has brought its measure of personal pain and isolation for me, but I have resorted to my upbringing and the lessons I learned there about family and community strength.

African Americans in predominantly white institutions often experience the phenomena of marginality as it relates to being isolated on campus (Turner, 2002). The first few years of my existence at the college were spent lamenting over the loneliness of being the only African American-female in administration. Before coming here, I had worked at a large community college in New York City where the faculty was quite diverse. I was used to seeing faces like mine and was mentored by a strong Jamaican faculty member who taught me how to maneuver and negotiate my way through the academic maze. It was quite a challenge for me to now be in a place with so few black faces. About a week after I began my job, a colleague from another institution gave me a bit of advice that was priceless and helped me to significantly lessen the isolation that I felt. He told me that my "on" campus survival would depend on my "off" campus involvement with people of color in the community. I took that advice and became actively involved in both the community that I live in as well as the one surrounding the college. That involvement led me to befriend an older African-American woman from the community who still greets me with, "How are you doing, dear? You just let me know if they're not treating you right up there, okay." That cryptic greeting speaks volumes and has gotten me through many trying times over the past ten years.

Getting support from "community" is definitely a way to lessen the isolation that one encounters when placed in a predominantly white environment. I learned this as a teenager growing up in Harlem. My whole world was black. Even the nuns who taught in the school were black. It was not until I reached the eighth grade and applied to high school that my world began to expand. I expected that I would attend a high school that was close to my home. However, the principal took the liberty of adding schools that none of us had ever heard of to my application list. Subsequently, when I received my acceptance notifications, both my parents and I were shocked. The principal convinced not just my parents but also those of many of my classmates that she had our best interest at heart. That year she sent most of us off to places far beyond our comfort zones. Although many of us did not know it at the time, being smart and black would mean that we would be "blessed" with a sense of isolation that we simply were not prepared for (Fries-Britt, 1998). I ultimately went to an all-girls, all-white school in the Bronx. On my first day at the new school, I remember wishing that I could have attended a school where at least some of the faces were familiar. In my freshman class of 203 students, there were two African Americans and one Puerto Rican. Thus in 1966, I began the journey into the volatile world of integration. I received an inordinate amount of support from my family during those days, much like the support that I get today from the community around the college. I know that I would never have survived had it not been for the positive affirmations that I received at home. Likewise, I would not have gotten through the last ten years at this institution had it not been for the community's support.

During my sophomore year in high school, Martin Luther King, Jr., was killed, and the uprisings that occurred in Harlem could not hold a candle to the searing racism that I experienced in high school. My English teacher announced that the people who participated in the riots were animals and that I should make it my mission to prove to my classmates, and the world for that matter, that I was different that the rest of "them." That statement will remain with me for the rest of my life. What she said, albeit indirectly, was that "we've let you into our world, so don't let us see you associate with the disenfranchised masses. Leave them alone and assimilate." I remember asking her, "What do you mean by them?" She never answered me but chose instead to proceed with the day's lesson. I, on the other hand, learned a different lesson that day. It is a lesson that black faculty members can learn as well. Never let anyone dupe you into believing that you must stand alone and separate yourself from the rest of "them." Unfortunately, many whites on our campuses are uncomfortable when they see two or more black people talking together. African-American males are even more suspect when they are seen together (Flowers, 2003). Don't be afraid to get together with other people of color both on and off campus. Believe it or not, there really isn't anything wrong with faculty of color "sitting together in the cafeteria!" (Tatum, 1997)

Obviously God was not concerned about my comfort level when He placed me in that high school or at the institutions of higher learning in which I have worked. In both situations, I spent a tremendous amount of valuable time looking at the grass that I thought was greener on the other side. God had a plan, and thankfully He did not choose to answer my prayer to "remove" me to "higher grounds" until He was ready. God used the adversity that I experienced to create a blessing for me. God anoints you in trouble, not from trouble. When I took on the new position as Dean, which I was somewhat reluctant to take, African-American women in leadership positions were not always given the respect that they should have. Although I still spend much energy teaching other faculty members how to transcend their own limitations and prejudices as it relates to our students, I know I am making a difference in both the institution and the students I serve. God never brings you to a place to leave you. He will bring people and resources that you need to get the job done. He has not failed me yet.

I have come to the realization that the term Christian College is not necessarily synonymous with heaven on earth. Although I was thankful that we all had Jesus in common, the fact still remained that God was not and is not finished with any of us. There simply were no "angel wings" to be found on the campus. Change would inevitably come, and God would keep me there long enough to see the positive changes that only He could have orchestrated.

Tips for Survival

My prayer partner of over 20 years was having an exceedingly difficult time at the bank where she worked. She told me about a sermon that she had heard by T.D. Jakes entitled "The Ten Commandments of Working in a Hostile Environment." It blessed her so much that I decided to get a copy for myself. Many of its principles have provided me with useful spiritual and practical steps to follow:

I make sure that I pray before I leave home in the morning. T.D. Jakes speaks a great deal about being "fully armored" when you leave for work. Just like you wouldn't leave your house in the morning without clothes on, you should never leave without earnest prayer. I can work with bees, snakes, and even anthrax if I am properly clothed, and so it goes with being prepared for working in a challenging environment.

I stopped seeing adversity as a problem. The more I am challenged, the more I become energized. Since I don't know everything, I tend to seek the advice of other professionals, both on and off campus, when looking to find a resolution for a problem.

I learned that being loved is a wonderful thing, but it is not a requirement to get the job done. When I stand up for righteousness and justice on behalf of the students that I serve, I am bound to face some level of resistance. Many of us were hired to be role models for these students. The next generation of students needs to see us as strong adults with righteous convictions. The students will surely benefit, and my colleagues will respect the fact that we stand for a cause. Believe it or not, no one likes an Uncle Tom (or Aunt Thomasina for that matter). Forget about being on the "I'm not trying to lose my good job" plan. If God brought you to an institution, He will keep you there until it is time for you to go. Satan cannot do any more to you than God will allow, as it happened with his servant Job!

It is not wise to avoid people who don't like me. Those people may be just the key to my blessing. Who knows, I may be the key to theirs.

God has given me gifts, strengths, and talents. I have developed more than one if for no other reason than to honor Him. This has broadened my outlook and my résumé.

Throughout the past decade I have dealt with resistance, readjusted expectations, and learned a few survival techniques along the way. God has been faithful and kept me at my present institution long enough to know that "I can do all things through God who strengthens me" (Philippians 4:13).

References

Alfred, M. V., "Reconceptualizing Marginality from the Margins: Perspectives of African American Tenured Female Faculty at a White Research University," *The Western Journal of Black Studies, 25(1)*, (2001).

Brown, L. M. and Dobbins, H., "Students' of Color and European American Students' Stigma-Relevant Perceptions of University Instructors," *Journal of Social Issues, 60(1)*, (2004).

Flowers, L. A., & Jones, L., "Exploring the Status of Black Male Faculty Utilizing Data from the National Study of Postsecondary Faculty," *The Journal of Men's Studies, 12(1)*, (2003).

Fries-Britt, S., "Moving beyond Black Achiever Isolation: Experiences of Gifted Black Collegians," *Journal of Higher Education, 69(5)*, (1998).

Jackson, J. F., "Toward Administrative Diversity: An analysis of the African-American Male Educational Pipeline," *The Journal of Men's Studies, 12(1)*, (2003).

Jackson, R. L. and Crawley, R. L., "White Student Confessions about a Black Male Professor: A Cultural Contracts Theory Approach to Intimate Conversations about Race and Worldview," *The Journal of Men's Studies, 12(1)*, (2003).

Mitchell, I. A., "Honors Programs at Historically Black Colleges and Universities," *Education, 123(1)*, (2002).

Journal of Blacks in Higher Education, "Black Enrollments at the Nation's Christian Colleges Are on the Rise," (Spring, 2004).

Tatum, B. D. *Why Are All the Black Kids Sitting Together in the Cafeteria?* (New York: Basic Books, 1997).

Thompson, C. J. and Dey, E. L., "Pushed to the Margins: Sources of Stress for African American College and University Faculty," *Journal of Higher Education, 69(3)*, (1998).

Turner, C. S., "Women of Color in Academe: Living with Multiple Marginality," *Journal of Higher Education, 73(1)*, (2002).

Nell Lewis

Nell Lewis, humanitarian, author, and retired educator, was born in Jamesville, NC. She was among the first African-American students to integrate Jamesville High School in 1965. Ms. Lewis received her undergraduate degree (French, 1972) and graduate degree (School Administration, 1987) from East Carolina University. Her educational career included an equal number of years in the classroom and in school administration.

Ms. Lewis's legacy to post-Civil Rights generations is her book *1 Day and 3 Hours,* which is a riveting story of her journey of faith in the workplace since integration. Her story brings to life the remarkable power within each one of us to overcome the lingering challenges of race relations.

Among many noted accomplishments, Ms. Lewis was named the 2003 recipient of the Best-Irons Humanitarian Award for her distinctive service in promoting community unity.

She was executive producer and host of the university sponsored TV show "Diversity Moments with Nell," which aired for three years as a part of her programming features while she served as Director of the Ledonia Wright Cultural Center at East Carolina University. She hosted 30-minute exclusive interviews with Carl Brashear, whose life story is told in the movie *Men of Honor,* and Herman Boone, whose life story is told in the movie *Remember the Titans.*

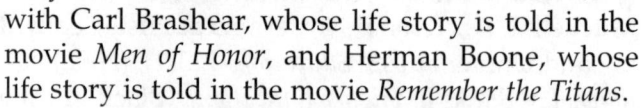

Ms. Lewis speaks on college campuses and in business forums as well as in churches, community, and during family events. Many lives are touched and changed through her contagious enthusiasm for living life's eternal quality in everyday situations.

Her prophetic revelation about the matter of race is a chilling conclusion: If we don't willingly embrace our common humanity, we will be forced to in a moment of common helplessness.

1 Day and 3 Hours

Nell Lewis

Against the backdrop of 21st century America, questions still surface around man's inhumanity to man. At 14 years of age, when my elementary school principal made the announcement to me on a spring day in 1965 that I would be "sent" to the white high school the next year, I began my own search for answers to understanding this senseless notion that we can regard any other human being less than ourselves. This would be a defining moment which would set my life on a course that nearly 40 years later finds me wrestling with just as many thoughts and questions about man's inhumanity to man as I had then. Sadly, these questions stem from my experiences and observations in the world of academia where true enlightenment should ultimately be taught and embraced.

My story reveals a sobering reality of the lingering challenges of race relations, and it gives a stark warning of the peril many among our post-Civil Rights generations will likely encounter if they are not anchored in the most powerful human legacy—a strong heritage of faith.

On February 15, 2003, three years after I became director of a cultural center on a university campus in North Carolina, I was named the recipient of the Best-Irons Humanitarian Award given each year to a local citizen for outstanding work in building "community" around human relations. As I was presented the award, a great deal of the recognition mentioned was for the work I had accomplished at the university's cultural center. The following week, congratulatory notes, letters, emails, and phone calls poured into my office from national, state, and local educators, politicians, students, alumni, and others.

After being named the recipient of the Best-Irons Humanitarian Award, what happened just a few weeks later is still unconscionable to so many university faculty, staff, and students as well as members of the local community, not to mention many on the national level who had come to hear about this university cultural center for the first time just three years prior when I became its new director. I received what I considered at the time to be a routine phone call on April 1, 2003, from an administrative assistant who informed me as she had countless times before that her boss would like to see me in his office. The date she gave me for the meeting was April 3rd (two days later) at 2:00 p.m.

Thursday, April 3, 2003, began just like any ordinary day. There was nothing unusual about that morning. The weather was as pleasant as ever. I was still feeling, as my student workers were, the exuberance of a successful year on the job. The court of public opinion was in. Resoundingly, the students, staff, faculty, and community had declared another stellar year for the university's cultural center! A place with little to no name recognition even on the campus when I assumed the position of director had come to be revered as a lighthouse of hope for leading the charge toward cultural enlightenment and connection in the ever-increasing global climate of our university and community. No one knew like I did that the success that was on our heels was because I had learned the secret, which is to start each day in total dependence on God, asking for His strength, His wisdom, and His revelation. I made this request each day. So this morning was not unlike any other morning in which, before leaving for work, I held up representative communion elements (bread and grape juice), acknowledging the power each represented through the blood of Jesus and His broken body. After a few moments spent talking to and listening to God, I partook of the elements. The Holy Spirit of God, knowing in advance the strength and revelation I would need on this day, had prompted me some four months ago to begin each day with Holy Communion. I had obeyed. The precious Holy Spirit knows how to strengthen us for battle! I did not realize the height, width, or depth of the power that God was building up in me until the afternoon of this very day, April 3, 2003.

A few minutes before 2:00 p.m., with my meeting portfolio in hand and exhilarated by its contents, which was a final report on the success of the last two signature programs for the year, I informed my staff that I was off to the meeting that the administrative assistant had scheduled two days prior. Some of us had been busy all morning putting the final touches on these reports for two major events that the cultural center had just sponsored. The first was the African American Firsts program with Master Chief Carl Brashear as the keynote speaker. His life story is told in the movie Men of Honor. The other major event was an African-American Health Summit with keynote speaker Dr. Joycelyn Elders, former Surgeon General. I wanted to share these successes with the administrator when I went to the 2:00 meeting. This was our routine whenever we met. He would share with me what was on his mind about the cultural center and other things going on around campus, and I would share with him an update on the progress my staff and I were making. I had all of this information neatly placed in my meeting portfolio as I left for his office close to 2:00 p.m. that Thursday.

Entering the administrator's office, I noticed a second party, another administrator who was an assistant to a higher-level administrator, seated at the table. Instantly I knew this was not a routine meeting. The administrator with whom I had been scheduled to meet handed me a copy of an email, and for some reason my eyes fell first on the date and time it had been sent—April 3, 2003 at 2:00 p.m. I thought there must be some significance between this email and my being asked to meet here at the same time that someone pushed a Send button to send this email throughout our campus. The major subject of the email was that an Office of Equity and Diversity was being established. I would understand why this was so significant by the end of this meeting. The administrator asked me if I had seen that email. I informed him that I had not. He then told me to read it. I wondered how he expected that I had seen this email, which was sent at 2:00 today, when I am meeting with him in his office at 2:00 today. He continued talking as I tried to skim over the contents of the email, which immediately revealed the motive behind this meeting. The administrator in his office with us, noticing that it was difficult for me to try to skim the email and listen to him talk at the same time, said to him in a rather stern and what I considered an authoritative voice, "Let her read that first. She can't read and listen to you at the same time." He replied in a rather submissive and seemingly ashamed tone, "Okay." I thoroughly read each line, and I looked up when I had finished.

The administrator then began again by saying to me, "As you know, my boss (referring to his boss) has been re-engineering and reorganizing the campus, and you are being reassigned from the cultural center over to the library as an outreach coordinator." After making this statement and seeing no reaction from me, he went on to ask, "How do you feel about this?" I answered in a soft almost whispering tone (carefully enunciating each word), "I don't know how I feel about this. I'm hearing it for the first time right now, so I don't know how I feel about this." Obviously confounded by how calm and unmoved I seemed to be, he asked, "Do you understand?" I answered again carefully enunciating each word as I had done to his last question, "Yes, I understand. This is clear, real clear; in fact, it is crystal (with emphasis) clear." At those words both administrators looked confounded and speechless, almost as if my peace and calm response had made them lose track of the "script." To help them regroup as I observed their puzzled look (over my calmness), I said looking at one and then at the other, "It looks like you two are waiting for something." I could tell I was reading the situation perfectly because their lips moved simultaneously in a subconscious-like motion to try to utter some kind of follow up that wouldn't immediately come. Trying not to have me notice their shock at the mystery of my calmness, the administrator that had called the meeting, regaining his composure, went on to give me the end of the script, "This change is effective Monday, April 7." I nodded my head indicating only that I had heard what he said. In my mind, I was thinking, "What's the big rush? Why is it so important that this reassignment take place so abruptly?" Only 1 day and 3 hours to shut down what had become the zenith of the cultural center's existence and to close the door on what had become like my very next breath—my passion for the work of building an atmosphere charged with respect for the dignity and worth of all human beings of all cultures and ethnic groups.

The administrator's next words which followed my nod were obviously purposefully and well thought through. He continued, "I want you to be sure that you don't let anybody know how you feel about this." I calmly responded (still under the powerful influence of the Holy Spirit, who had really been speaking through me the whole time), "You don't have to worry about that, but I can't control anyone else expressing how they feel about this," to which the administrator replied, "Oh, I know. I know." It was clear that, knowing my passion for the work I did, both administrators in this meeting had expected me to lose my composure. I have to tell this each time I tell this story: I never knew until that Thursday in this administrator's office just how BIG God (His Holy Spirit) really does live in me. I thank God for the privilege of knowing.

The spirit of discernment brought into clear focus for me the significance of the email that I had been asked to read at the outset of this meeting announcing the establishment of an Office of Diversity and Equity, which was sent across campus as I sat in this meeting. Up to this moment, I had been the undeniable champion of diversity on our campus as reflected in the major focus of the campus and community for their diversity needs. This new "Office of Diversity and Equity"—what was the significance of its establishment on the same date and time as my reassignment? Could it be that some "good faith" move was deemed necessary to try to suggest that diversity would still be in good hands as the word would begin to spread that the undeniable "champion of diversity" was being reassigned?

After leaving this meeting, I walked up the steps of the cultural center and turned the knob knowing that the most difficult part of this day would take place on the other side of the door where my student workers had already assembled around the table for a staff meeting to begin plans for the programs and activities for the next academic year! As I entered the room, the students were excitedly going over some work details. As they stopped to recognize my entrance into the room and to yield to my place on the agenda, I encouraged them to continue their discussion and told them I would get to my part of the agenda later. I really intended to do that, but as I saw the excitement with which they were making future plans, I could not let them continue what I knew would not happen, not now anyway. So I interrupted and began to tell them about the meeting I had just left. Their faces went blank. Some shook their heads in disbelief; others began to trickle one tear, then another and another as I tried to encourage them by reflecting on the good we had done. I assured them that our legacy would live on in the minds of this campus and community. Nothing could change that. By now, each face revealed the weight of what so many would come to call a "senseless act." They sat there at length—speechless—heads shaking—as if hoping I would say at some point, "I'm just joking." I could read in the students' faces that they were asking themselves, "What had been the use of the hard work and sacrifices?" I could also sense that they were asking themselves, "What kind of society are we coming to?" These students would later express their thoughts in the student newspaper (*The East Carolinian*).[1]

After watching the mounting expressions of shock and disbelief for about two hours, I said, "Come on, we've got a lot of packing to do." Like the troopers they were, I heard them discussing who would do what and where they would start, mixed with comments about how senseless this was. Only a little packing time was left after the staff meeting. After all, it was only about three hours ago that I learned the news of my reassignment. That left the next day—one day—to finish the packing and pull the shade on what had seemed like a three-year marathon! (One) 1 day and 3 hours seemed awfully unusual. I would hear in the days ahead many students, staff, faculty, and members of the community express the "1 day and 3 hours" conclusion that they had reached: the "rush" was to make this a done deal before too many students or members of the community got wind of it because that would most likely mean a protest to disable the plans of those responsible for reassigning me.

In the meantime, some of the key administrators involved in my being reassigned were themselves reassigned and even dismissed a few months after I began working at the library. This came as quite a shock to our campus. Nothing like this had ever happened before. I might add that these administrators had about as little notice of the change in their position as I had been given.

I am now retired after serving only nine months in the reassigned position. As I look back to my walking on the grounds of the all-white high school in 1965, I can now connect the dots from that point to my retirement and see how other such challenging experiences after that equipped me with divine strength, wisdom, and revelation to triumph over my 1 day and 3 hour experience. "Now thanks be unto God, which always causeth us to triumph in Christ." [2]

For the sake of our post-Civil Rights generations, may our moral conscience awaken us to this reality: If we do not willingly embrace our common humanity, we will be forced to in a moment of common helplessness.

Source Notes

1. Hicks, Natausha et al., "Letter to the Editor," *The East Carolinian*, April 17, 2003 Vol. 79 No. 72 A4.
2. II Corinthians 2:14, King James Version. *Holy Bible* (KJV).

Stephen K. Appiah-Padi

Dr. Stephen K. Appiah-Padi has a doctoral degree in Educational Policy and Administration with a specialization in international/intercultural education from the University of Alberta, Edmonton, Canada. He has also had training and certification as Appreciative Inquiry Facilitator (2004), in Online Teaching (MVU, 2003), New Science Leadership (2003), Leadership in Inclusive (Diversity) Breakthrough (2003), Multicultural Course Transformation (2002), and Quality Management (2002).

Dr. Appiah-Padi has worked in various capacities with international and multicultural students and is currently the Director of Diversity and Intercultural Education at Lansing Community College. He has more than 10 years of teaching experience in both 4- and 2-year higher education institutions. In his current position, he works with faculty and staff for multicultural curricular transformation and cultural competence. In this capacity, he has created and facilitated several workshops for faculty in the community college. He has also facilitated a monthly faculty and staff dialogue circle on various diversity-related topics. Dr. Appiah-Padi created the TIPS model of diversity teaching, which focuses on building relationships through dialogue in the community college classroom.

In the community, Dr. Appiah-Padi serves on the Greater Lansing Commission on Race and Ethnicity (city of Lansing) and the International Services Committee of the American Red Cross, as well as board membership of the Capital Area Center for Independent Living (for people with disabilities).

Alone and Assailed in the Heartland of America

Stephen K. Appiah-Padi, Ph.D.

Do not gloat over me, my enemies! For though I fall, I will rise again. Though I sit in darkness, the Lord himself will be my light. (Micah 7:8)

I have never been afraid to be a minority. In fact, all my life I have thrived best in minority situations. Growing up in Ghana, West Africa, I rarely lived in the locality where I was born. Much of my education was in towns and cities far from my hometown. Further education has taken me to England, precisely to a little college town in midwest England called Loughborough, and to Edmonton, Alberta, Canada. On countless occasions during these sojourns, I have been conscious of but never afraid of my minority status.

So in August of 1999, when I loaded my 1995 Plymouth voyager minivan with all the possessions I had acquired in Canada and headed south to take up a teaching/administrative position in a college in northwest Iowa, I had no fears at all. When a good neighbor in Canada heard that I was moving to the United States, he mustered up the courage to tell me he thought I was making a mistake. "Have you not heard about all the racism in the U.S.?" he asked with a pleading demeanor in his eyes. I courteously dismissed his concern, trusting that I had enough experience to survive in whatever environment I lived. So to Iowa I went.

My new position was at a college which since its establishment in 1882 had never had a black faculty or administrator. I was to be the first black professor to teach there. Luckily for me though, another black professor was hired a month or so after I got there. This brought the number of black families in the town to three. Here we were, a grand total of 15 black folk, counting spouses and children, floating in a sea of about 5,000 white faces.

To make matters more interesting, I learned after I got there that the vice president of Academic Affairs (VPAA) of the college who hired me, and who was to be my supervisor, was moving to another college. And so also was the president of the college. Thus, the two people I had had serious discussions with before my appointment were no longer going to be there. I was, however, assured by them that their successors would also be deeply committed to diversity.

During my first year I worked under the supervision of an interim VPAA, a retired professor of the college who was brought back from retirement to hold the fort until a substantive VPAA was appointed. The presidency was also to be shared temporarily, between him and the vice president of finance. Indeed, these two gentlemen were compassionate, understanding, and, to a large extent, very supportive of me. Although the year was one of learning for me, it also was a very fruitful one. I felt appreciated and welcomed by the college community. I had a free hand to do what I needed to do, and my work produced results. The honeymoon ended with the appointment of the new VPAA. She came on board in August 2000, and her entrance marked the beginning of a horrid experience which nothing in my past could have prepared me for.

As I look back on the two years I spent under this woman, I can see a well-orchestrated plan of deliberate criticism and insidious vilification of everything I stood for. For most people of color on predominantly white campuses, the major cause of discomfort is the hostile environments they are made to endure. Such environments are sometimes deliberately created and manipulated to undermine their effectiveness. My story details some of the tricks used to foster hostile working environments for people of color— lack of clear supervisory direction, exaggeration of shortcomings to justify criticism, and strategic acts of undermining. I relate my experience here for the purpose of letting other brothers and sisters who tread professional paths in predominantly white colleges to be conscious of the sudden twists and turns that are common in these environments. The earlier one is able to recognize signs of anti-black agenda on a campus, the sooner can one begin to confront it.

Muddying the Waters

Organizational development experts emphasize the importance of trust in managing change at the workplace. While workers look to managers to provide direction for the organization, workers trust that such direction is, in the least, taken to advance the organization's goals. Trust is eroded when the direction is not forthcoming or is deliberately clouded. Worse still is when the direction mapped out by a not-so-well-meaning supervisor is meant to trap subordinates into failure; something is seriously amiss.

I remember at my first meeting with the new vice president of Academic Affairs (I will subsequently refer to her as the dean). She told me she wanted to ease my workload because she felt the tasks covered by the International Programs director (my position) were too extensive. She told me she had decided to create an associate dean position to assume some of the tasks. I did not know if I had any say in that, but I was happy with the move because of my excess workload. In addition to my duties as director of International Programs, which included recruitment and retention of international and minority students, curricular internationalization, study abroad programs, and a number of programming duties in between, I also taught six credits for the Education department. A memo from the dean's office a week later announced the appointment of one of the faculty as associate dean "to oversee off-campus programs." I soon discovered that, rather than assuming some of my tasks, the associate dean position was to become another supervisory level between the dean and me. It essentially was meant to cut off my direct access to the dean. When I was hired, my contract indicated that I was to report to the dean.

The responsibility "to oversee off-campus programs" was never fully explained. I asked the associate dean what it meant in relation to my responsibilities. His answer was always to throw the question back to me to determine what my job was. So I never had a job description. I found myself in a situation where I was always accused of not doing my job well, yet my supervisors never bothered to define the job they expected me to do. For the time that the associate dean was "overseer of off-campus programs," his office only produced criticisms of my work, nothing by way of advice or direction that one might expect from a supervisor. The one and only administrative evaluation of me in this position was never discussed with me, as is clearly directed on the evaluation form, yet criticisms were leveled at virtually everything I did. I came to the conclusion that the associate dean position was created strategically to put obstacles in my way and to put a white face in the International Programs Department.

Criticize, Criticize, Criticize

Charles Schwab once wrote: "In my wide association in life, meeting with many and great men in various parts of the world, I have yet to find the man, however great or exalted his station, who did not do better work and put forth greater effort under a spirit of approval than he would ever do under a spirit of criticism." I have always been aware that no one who wanted to rise above the ordinary has ever escaped criticism, so I do not have an aversion for criticism. Yet the kind and nature of criticism I endured under my dean and her assistant were clearly meant to ensure I was unsuccessful in my position.

As director of International Programs, I managed the college's annual summer institute. In the summer of 2000, I organized the institute with success. For the first time in many years, the institute turned a profit and many of the students went on to enroll in the fall. I was commended by the interim VPAA and interim president for my good work. Yet midway through the 2001 institute, the associate dean, who had previously not shown any interest in being directly involved with the institute, started raising questions about my leadership of it. He accused me of not properly communicating with other departments in the college. He was very hostile and insinuated that the program was in crises. When I asked him for specifics, he was evasive. When I pressed him further, he suggested that we go to talk to the dean together. That meeting with the dean and the associate dean was the single worst incident in my life at this college (August 23, 2001). I faced a two-hour barrage of criticism upon criticism and some having no factual basis, some on assumptions that were clearly stereotypical and perhaps even racist.

When criticism is merely meant to tear down and not to correct, it takes no cognizance of effort. At the beginning of one academic year when I made a plan of activities for the semester, I discussed everything with the associate dean. I remember him telling me how wonderful the plan was and even added a few suggestions of his own. One particular initiative would involve the general student population, so I thought the best way to get the message across was to have a story written about it in the student newspaper. When this story was published, the dean was angry. She complained that the story was published without "anybody's" input. Surprisingly, the associate dean, with whom I had discussed the program before having it publicized, also denied ever knowing about it. In fact, the publication attracted a lot of attention among students, many of whom volunteered for the initiative. Not even that success story could abate the dean's anger toward me. It became clear to me that the real reason she was angry was because I was succeeding and that was contrary to her desires.

Strategic Undermining

When detractors' words fail to break you down, watch out for subtle changes in process and procedures to undermine your authority. And they surely did come. In many different ways, my privileges, even rights, were withdrawn with impunity; my subordinates were favored over me, and I was marginalized as if I never existed.

Various aspects of my job were taken away from me without notice. First it was my budget. Monthly budget reports from the finance office stopped coming to me. The dean instructed the staff at the financial office to send the reports to the associate dean. Without any notice to me, the dean decided to allow a part-time international student counselor in my office to go on a recruitment trip to Korea and Japan instead of me. I had made this trip two years before with very impressive results in terms of recruitment. When I later found out and asked the associate dean about it, he explained that the dean had made the decision, with the reason that the student "was the natural person to recruit from the Pacific Rim because she comes from Taiwan and had contacts there." I was later asked to assist her with my contacts list and to prepare her for the trip because she had no experience in recruiting.

During my tenure, I was on a 9-month contract. Yet the nature of the summer institute I directed was such that I had to work all year round. When I asked for this to be rectified, the dean insisted there was no money to pay for it. I resigned in May 2002, and, barely a month later, the position was restructured into a 12-month position and given to a white male confidant of the dean. An assistant director was also appointed to help him. Significantly, the associate dean was no longer going to oversee the position which now reported directly to the dean. The desired face had been put in place, so there was no longer a need for a "white" overseer.

Conclusion

During such harrowing experiences, if you have no one to talk to and cannot find a sound way out, you may be driven to extremes. In my case, I endured very stressful times. I came close to breakdown several times. After one of those meetings of criticism, I was very distraught and while driving home I thought: "Why isn't anybody here listening to me? What can I do to stop this harassment?" I thought about driving my car into a tree by the roadside to draw attention to my pain. But the good Lord intervened. I remember hearing something close to the words of Micah 8:7, "Though you fall, you will rise again." And I drove on home into the loving arms of my wife and children.

I did not see it coming and I had no plan when it came. To any person of color on a predominantly white campus, my first advice is to stay connected to a community of black people as well as truly

Alone and Assailed in the Heartland of America

caring white folk. There might be white people in such environments who have some genuine love to share. Find them and connect with them. I don't know what I would have done if I did not have the few souls around who listened and comforted me. I had not heard about JDOTT when I was in Iowa, otherwise I would certainly have connected. I made frantic attempts to seek out a black pastor who lived about an hour from me. He was helpful, but I found him a little too late—after I had decided to quit. It is also important that you keep your eyes open for suspicious treatment. It is easy to feel useless if criticism is your boss's main communication style, but it helps if you are also able to see a discriminatory pattern of behavior towards you. Once you lose your ability to discern abuse, you lose the power to challenge it and you unwittingly succumb to it. One way of recognizing the pattern earlier is through reflection and journaling. Reflecting on individual incidents enables you to see connections and to understand situations better.

Without any doubt to me, the most potent protection I had against my situation was my faith. I never stopped asking the Lord for wisdom and guidance. And indeed He provided, for how else could I be sane enough today to tell this story? Despite the hostile work environment, the Lord provided a loving church for worship. All the emotional aches and pains accumulated Monday through Friday were assuaged on Sundays. The pastor of my church became a good friend to me. He was the caring, uplifting soul who the Lord sent to soothe my wounds. He prayed with me several times, and he gave me godly advice. Yes, he is white, but he could see beyond the color of my skin and recognize a human being who needed comfort. Anytime I look back on this sojourn in Iowa, I cannot forget what the Lord did for me through this pastor.

Now that the Lord has given me safe passage from "Egypt," and has enabled me to rise again, I look to Him to deliver me from all troubles. My current job environment is much better, but it is still a predominantly white campus. What the Lord has taught me about trusting Him is to never let my guard down. I have this poem in my office to remind me of that:

> God is too good to be unkind
> God is too wise to be confused
> When I cannot trace His hand
> I can trust His heart.

Pamela Mitchell-Crump

Dr. Pamela Mitchell-Crump is Associate Dean of Academic Finance and Assistant to the Senior Vice President of Academic Affairs at Westfield State College, located in Westfield, Massachusetts. She has worked in the area of human resource management for over 21 years and has an extensive background in equal opportunity and diversity.

Dr. Mitchell-Crump received a bachelor of science degree in Justice and Law Administration from Western Connecticut State University and a masters of public administration in Public Law and Management from the University of Hartford. She received a doctorate of education in Higher Education Administration from the University of Massachusetts at Amherst. She has also completed Harvard University's Management Development Program.

Dr Mitchell-Crump's research interests include higher education administration, institutional diversity, and women of color in academe.

Know Your Place or No You May Not

Pamela Mitchell-Crump, Ph.D.

It was August 1997. The college had a new president, and all were hopeful that he would bring about positive changes. As director of the Equal Opportunity Office, my primary concern was about the new president's general commitment to equal opportunity and affirmative action. Secondly, I was concerned about his support of the office that oversaw these two functional areas. The Equal Opportunity Office had always reported directly to the president of the college because of the importance of its function and the need for that function not to be compromised.

In December of that year, it came to my attention through another department head that the Equal Opportunity Office would no longer report directly to the president's office and that the office would be combined with the Human Resources Office. I questioned why I had not been told this directly by the president. After all, I still worked directly for him. Nonetheless, I proceeded to set up a meeting with the president. I hoped he would deny or confirm what I had been told.

The Initial Meeting

The meeting day with the president had come. I shared what I had been told only to receive confirmation. I then asked why I had not been consulted or at least informed directly by him. I was met with a deafening look as if to say, "I didn't feel that was necessary" and "your input does not matter anyway." Shocked and disappointed, I proceeded to provide a brief history of myself and the human resources department head and pointed out that a merger of the two offices could compromise the effectiveness of the Equal Opportunity Office. Once again, I was met with a deafening stare, this time accompanied by directives that the human resources department head and I were to "work out the details." I politely excused myself and ended our meeting. On the walk back to my office I was, needless to say, upset. I now had more questions than I did going into the president's office. I questioned what I had done or not done to make the president want to make such a change. I kept wrestling with the question of why the president had not consulted me about the change but had met and consulted with the department head of the area to which I and my assistant would now be reporting. I then begin to realize that this was an issue of power and control that was acutely impacted by race. As an African-American female administrator within a predominantly white institution, I was seen as having too much power, control, and autonomy. After all, as an African American and a female who was in the administrative ranks of a predominantly white institution, I should be grateful for the privilege to be there, right?

What Is the Problem?

There were a number of issues that would make the merging of the equal opportunity and the human resources offices difficult. Many of the reasons were self-evident; others were more subtle and would only be known to select staff within the two areas. There were three obvious reasons. The first was the fact that a director headed human resources and I was also a director heading equal opportunity. Thus, how can one supervise someone who has the same title and same level as themselves? This issue seemed to be of no concern to anyone but me. Maybe me being an African American and a female and the director of human resources being a Caucasian male was all the justification that was needed. Was I to consider him my supervisor versus a colleague? In my mind, the answer was clearly the latter and not the former. The larger issue was the fact that the equal opportunity officer, according to the state's Equal Opportunity/Affirmative Action/Diversity Plan for State Public Higher Education Institutions, was to report directly to the president.

The second obvious issue revolved around the fact that the majority of situations that came to the attention of the Equal Opportunity Office—equal opportunity, affirmative action, and disparate treatment—were confidential and were not the concern of Human Resources. In fact, many matters and complaints raised were the direct result of decisions made by Human Resources. Thus, I was being placed in a situation of needing to conduct confidential business without my supposed supervisor having any idea of what I was doing, and it was difficult.

Third and most important was the fact that the functions of the Equal Opportunity Office would be severely compromised by being physically located within Human Resources. Individuals having concerns would have to physically enter the human resources area to make a complaint.

A less obvious reason the merger would not be effective was the fact that on numerous occasions in the past I tried to work with the director of human resources on a number of issues. These efforts were to no avail. I believed the director was intimidated by me because I always spoke my mind and always called him on something if I knew that what he was saying was not truthful or defensible. All the makings were present for a disastrous merger situation.

Efforts to Make a Bad Situation Workable

After many conversations with the human resource director about the details of the merger, it became crystal clear that this was not a merger of minds at all but, in fact, a dictatorship. I informed the president that there appeared to be no room for compromise on the part of the human resources director relative to the details of the merger. The president said he would talk to the director and get back to me. The president did get back to me all right. He made it crystal clear that things were going to be the way the human resources director wanted them and that the director had his full support. I realized then that I was just a pawn in a game in which I had no control.

And Then It Happened

I was called to the president's office. I thought it was to meet about an issue that I had been trying to meet with him about for the last few days. To my surprise, the meeting had been planned—a staged performance that obviously involved a rehearsal by the actors involved. As I walked into the president's office, he asked me to sit down. He told me he was going to ask his executive assistant to join us for the meeting. I could not figure out, for the life of me, why his executive assistant would need to join us. Then the president actually began to read to me a scripted piece from his desk which outlined the terms and conditions of my new assignment, the "merger," with human resources. Shocked, disappointed, and angry, I left the president's office in disbelief about what I had just experienced. I had been caught off guard, degraded, and been read to versus spoken with the president of the college about my reassignment in the presence of a witness, his executive assistant. Well, I'll be.

When I left work for the day, I shared what had happened to me with a trusted friend. As I talked about the situation and reflected on it, I was outraged. I decided to send the president a memorandum recapping what he had told me in the meeting and asking him some very pointed questions. I realized that even though he had shown me that he did not respect me nor could he care less about my thoughts, there was one thing he would understand and that was that I had a written accounting of the events that took place in his office on that very memorable afternoon.

From that day on I lost what little respect I had for him. I also decided that from then on, I would put everything I needed to say to him in memorandum form instead of affording him the courtesy of a conversation like most professionals do when dealing with their boss.

The Merger

It was during the fall of 1998 that my assistant and I were physically relocated to the human resources area, which was down the hall from where we were previously located. My assistant, however, was separated from me. She was housed in the central office of human resources, and I was in a separate office some 50 feet away. To add insult to injury, a division within human resources was subsequently relocated to our former office space that we had just been forced to vacate. Someone please explain this move to me.

Most days the environment was tense in human resources with very little collegiality. In my role as the equal opportunity and affirmative action officer, I had a reputation of being trustworthy and maintaining confidentiality for issues of discrimination (perceived or real) that were bought to my attention. As I had expected, shortly after the merger, members of the campus community came to me to express their concern about coming to speak to me in the new office location. If they scheduled an appointment with my assistant, individuals in human resources would know. If they came to see me directly, they took the chance of someone from human resources seeing them and assuming they were filing a complaint. As a result of the discomfort expressed, I began to offer to meet with people at a different location on campus, off campus, or even at their homes.

Other Functional Changes in the
Way Business Was Conducted

The way that I had conducted business for the past six and a half years had now changed. The interactions I had with my assistant had now changed. The interaction with key human resource staff were more frequent but nonetheless even more strained. I considered my new "boss" a colleague and not my supervisor since he and I had the same position level, "director." This alone caused some friction. I was not willing to be subservient nor would I ask permission for things. Don't get me wrong. I would share information that needed to be shared, but I was not asking to do things like most employees do of their supervisors. I had defined, for myself, my role and space within the box in which I had been placed. It was the only way I knew to remain sane and be effective in the position for which I had been hired and to which I was deeply committed and devoted.

The campus community needed someone to listen to their concerns about issues of discrimination, affirmative action, and disparate treatment. They needed someone who would do the right thing based upon getting the necessary information to make a well-informed, unbiased decision; someone who would maintain a delicate balance between working for the institution and representing the interests of the people of that institution.

One especially difficulty task was having to share information with the president about concerns that were raised about the human resources director, my supposed "boss" in such a way that the president would not interpret my informing him as going above the "boss's" head. This precarious situation is a key reason why the Equal Opportunity/Affirmative Action Office should always report directly to the president of a college. This, along with no longer having a direct and final decision about my assistant in a myriad of areas, was most upsetting. It was a difficult and challenging period of adjustment.

Like many African Americans, I generally do not complain about the different situations that happen in my life. I learn to deal with whatever hand is dealt to me knowing that the Lord makes no mistakes and everything that happens in life happens for a reason. After much prayer and meditation, I decided to be the bigger person and try to work with my supposed "boss" to accomplish some things that needed to be prepared/performed in order to make the college a better institution.

One such project was to establish a manual of hiring procedures which was desperately needed by the institution in an area that overlapped the role of human resources and equal opportunity. It was my hope that a collaborative effort from a number of key divisions on campus to establish such a manual would lay the groundwork for better working relationships. During the process of meeting with members on campus working within an established agenda to compose a hiring manual, I was met with a number of instances where Human Resources would be vocal about doing things a certain way which would essentially erase or significantly decrease the role that Equal Opportunity had in overseeing access and opportunity to all individuals who applied for positions at the college, particularly persons of color and women. Don't misunderstand me. It's okay to have differences of opinion as collaborators of a venture, but these differences should be hammered out and a resolution should be reached before presenting materials at a meeting with other departments on campus. This should particularly be expected when the materials were given to Human Resources to review before the meeting and no disagreement, concern, or constructive criticism was received from them. It is not okay for Human Resources to voice concerns in a meeting with other departments when we were to speak in one voice as collaborators of a joint venture.

After months of meetings and many hours of developing forms, procedures, and so forth, I decided to end the collaborative effort because it was not productive. It had become this turf/power issue—I am the boss, and this will work the way I want it to work despite the legal implications that were raised and despite the fact that the role of equal opportunity and affirmative action in hiring were perceived as much less important or even a nonissue for human resources. It had become an embarrassment for me.

Another major issue that the "boss" and I experienced was lack of communication. As his "assistant" (the title that was now added onto my directorship), he did not share with me departmental information that he received in meetings that I was not invited to attend. Nor did he share with me his thinking on day-to-day or longer term items and issues. How could I "assist" him if he did not talk to me? In fact, he only spoke to me when it was necessary or when it was obvious to others that he did not speak to me. This was particularly strange for me because I am a very approachable and easy-to-talk-to individual.

On many, many other occasions, I attempted to work with and talk to this man to get some things done. To no avail. I am a task-driven, organized individual, and he is a crisis-orientated, unorganized individual with very little follow-up and follow-through skills. Our styles were at opposite ends of the spectrum. This often proved to be disconcerting for me.

After some time of being patient and hoping for a change in heart of my colleague, I realized our relationship was not going to change. This realization forced me to conduct a serious introspection, looking at who I was and what I wanted to accomplish professionally.

That's the Way the Cookie Crumbles

The experiences of being combined with another department on campus, no longer having autonomy, and now having no direct reporting relationship with the university president was both detrimental professionally and negatively impacted me and my assistant personally. But who said academia would be a piece of cake? Who said that a president would find it necessary to consult with me about changes in the structure of a program that I oversaw? Who said that equal opportunity and affirmative action would be a priority and that necessary resources and support would be forthcoming by each succeeding president? Was I to take this personally as an African-American woman in the midst of an institution that was predominantly white and seemed to be intimidated by me? Whatever I thought, I had time to reflect on the situation and conduct some introspection.

I was in the final stages of a doctoral degree program and through my studies and working with different departments on campus had been exposed to the area of Academic Affairs. I began to look at how I could position myself to move to the administration area of academic affairs within this college or elsewhere.

Dealing with the Disappointment

A few secrets, if you will, that I would pass on to other African-American female administrators are:

Get a mentor—Find one or several individuals who will guide you, support you, and advise you as to how to handle situations that you will be confronted with as an administrator. Find someone you can confide in and someone whose opinion you respect. These individuals don't need to be female or African American.

Always be true to yourself—No matter what situation you may find yourself in, you cannot afford to sell your soul in order to be liked, to get that promotion you deserve, or to be like your colleagues and in good favor with the boss. As spiritual people, your conscience and the spirit within you will not be at peace if you allow those things that go against your upbringing or your very being to become a part of who you are.

Always stand your ground—Be firm and unwavering in the decisions you made based on having the appropriate information and weighing all the factors. People will have you second guessing yourself.

Always keep your options open—If your situation is an uncomfortable one, you will likely engage in searching for other positions. The more uncomfortable the situation, the more active your search becomes. I suggest that you be steadfast and constant. Look for, or at least be open to, new opportunities that may present themselves so that you are in a posture to receive them.

A New Day

After much stick-to-itiveness, I was able to receive a title change, move into the division of academic affairs, and have the opportunity to work with a true boss and colleague. There was mutual respect, and I learned new things.

There is often sunshine after the storm.

Epilogue

It is challenging to write an epilogue or conclusion to an unending saga. *Our Stories II* builds on experiences shared by the writers in our first book, *Our Stories*. The stories are different, but the underlying themes remain the same. The themes include problem areas that stem from racism, sexism, and other forms of discrimination; the impact or toll these negatives can have; the resiliency of black professionals; and the strategies that have been used to overcome and address the problems.

Problem Areas and Their Impact

The writers in *Our Stories II* have intimately shared their experiences in a way that captures the breadth and depth of experiences that often confront black professionals on predominantly white campuses. Regardless of whether the identified problems relate to obstacles in getting tenure and promotion, feelings of isolation and not belonging, or not being valued by colleagues, some black professionals perceive campus environments as being *exclusive* rather than *inclusive*. This means that they do not feel included in the mainstream of campus life or feel they have little input into important decisions that shape their institutions.

When institutions of higher education are permeated by racism and other negative "isms," faculty, staff, and students of color are often prevented from developing to their full potential. These negative situations cannot only thwart career aspirations and success, but can also take a toll emotionally, mentally, and physically. It is out of these negative experiences that we hear such statements and phrases such as "I have to work twice as hard in order to prove myself"; "They think I am here because of affirmative action, not because I am qualified"; or "I am sick and tired of being sick and tired." It is difficult to survive and remain in negative situations. Therefore, it is important for us note some of the strategies used to cope and/or change these situations.

Individual Strategies for Change

Usually when people find themselves in hostile or negative situations over a sustained period of time, they will adapt, fight, or flee. In other words, they will try to cope or change the situation or remove themselves from it. Some of our writers have provided suggestions that may help us cope or lighten our burden. Others told of the positive influence of mentors or other persons who advised and supported them. Some told of their efforts to change situations, and others told of their abilities to balance the various roles and demands placed on them. However, the role of spirituality, prayer, and their relationship to God was cited most often as being the ultimate source of their strength and survival. Much like our ancestors, the writers reveal their resiliency and ability to survive, thrive, and overcome obstacles in heroic fashion.

Collective Action as a Strategy for Change

Since the structural arrangements are similar at most predominantly white institutions, it would be most prudent for us to develop strategies to bring about institutional change. No one strategy will work in all situations because problems are situational and each institution has it own cultural configurations. However, institutions *can* and *do* change. Change may come from individual efforts or it may require collective action. In most instances, institutions change because it is in their best interest to do so. A historical example is when institutions of higher education integrated because the courts ruled that they must do so. Currently, it is interesting to see the number of colleges and universities that are changing race-based scholarships and other programs that were targeted for African Americans and other underrepresented groups because they want to avoid litigation.

Do institutions of higher education realize that it would be in their best interest to change the negative situations that confront African Americans and other people of color on their campuses? I contend that many institutions see the problems as individual troubles that can be address on a case by case basis. Therefore, symptoms are treated while the root of the problem persists and thus the cycle continues. However, when blacks organize themselves and speak as a collective voice, they often get the attention of the administration. The current need for collective action is not substantially different from the protest required during the Civil Rights Movement. For as long as racism and other forms of social injustice exist on predominantly white campuses, we need to come together with a unified voice and strategies that will result in desired outcomes. Thus there is a need for black faculty and staff organizations and/or organizations for people of color on these campuses.

One may ask what can be done when there are few blacks or people of color on campus or in the surrounding community and there are no allies to be found? It is out of awareness to these types of situations, that the need for a national organization to address the problems that confront black professionals on predominantly white campuses was born. We realized that an organized collective voice of many black professionals from predominantly white campuses across the country would wield more power to make systemic institutional change that can be sustained over time. No longer should we allow the perpetuation of racism, discrimination, prejudice, stereotypes, and inequities to be passed on from generation to generation. The John D. O'Bryant Think Tank (JDOTT) is committed to social justice and bringing about an institutional transformation that will allow blacks and other underrepresented groups to flourish and develop to their full potential. We encourage you to join us in becoming a part of the solution. Collectively, we can make a difference.

In conclusion, *Our Stories II* is a collection of real life experiences of black professionals on predominantly white campuses. It is our intent to use these personal situations as catalysts to heighten the awareness of issues and commit ourselves to work collectively to bring about needed change. As stakeholders in the academies of higher education, we must continue to provide support for each other but, more importantly, we must continue in the struggle until justice and equality prevails for blacks on predominantly white campuses.

About the Editors

Sherwood Smith

Dr. Sherwood Smith is Assistant Professor in the Human Development and Education Foundations Programs and serves out of the Provost's Office as the Director for the Center for Cultural Pluralism at the University of Vermont.

Previously he was a Post-Doctoral Fellow, with a dual appointment as Acting Assistant Director for the Office of Multicultural Affairs and Assistant to the Dean's Office for the College of Education and Social Services at the University of Vermont.

Dr. Smith has traveled extensively throughout the world. In the past he worked as a Peace Corps volunteer in Tanzania and was awarded the Outstanding Minority Returned Peace Corps Volunteer: 2001 National Award. He worked overseas as adjunct faculty for the School for International Training in Kenya. More recently he served as the Assistant Director of Residence Life at Penn State University. Dr. Smith's research has led to presentations for a variety of professional meetings and national conferences such as the National Conference on Multicultural Education and National Conference on Race & Ethnicity. He is a member of many other social justice and diversity organizations.

Dr. Smith's most recent publication is a chapter titled, "An Invisible Presence, Silenced Voices: African Americans in the Adult Education Professorate" in *Making Space Merging Theory to Practice in Adult Education*, which he co-authored with Dr. Scipio Colin III. Dr. Smith serves as one of the Northern representatives for JDOTT.

About the Editors

Mordean Taylor-Archer

Dr. Mordean Taylor-Archer received her Ph.D. in Social Policy, Planning & Administration from Brandeis University in 1979. She has a Master's in Sociology from the University of Arkansas and a Bachelor's in Social Science from the University of the Ozarks. She completed the Management Development Program at Harvard University in the summer of 1993.

She is currently the Vice Provost for Diversity and Equal Opportunity at the University of Louisville (began August 2001). Prior to this, she was Associate Provost for Diversity and Dual Career Development at Kansas State University (1990–2001).

She served as Assistant Dean of the School of Social Work at Virginia Commonwealth University (1983–1990), Assistant Professor and Field Work Coordinator, School of Social Work at Boston College (1975–1978), and Instructor at the School of Social Work at the University of Arkansas at Little Rock (1971–1974).

Dr. Taylor-Archer has received numerous awards including Outstanding Faculty Awards from Virginia Commonwealth University; Outstanding Administrator Award, Kansas State University; an appreciation award for founding the Kansas Association of African Americans in Higher Education; the Martin Luther King, Jr., Drum Major Award, Kansas State University; and The Barbara Jordan Leadership Award from the Big XII Council on Black Student Government. She received fellowships from the Herr for Human Rights, Brandeis University 1977–1978, and a Ford Foundation Fellowship for Graduate Study (1974–1977). She is listed in Who's Who Among African Americans and was selected as one of the most admired in the City of Manhattan, Kansas in January 2000. Dr. Taylor-Archer serves as Executive Vice President of JDOTT.

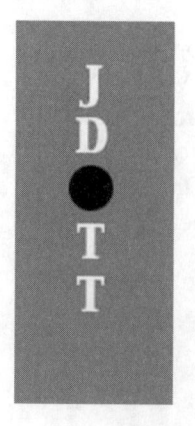

The JDOTT book emblem symbolizes the everlasting rippling effect of love that was exhibited by the late John D. O'Bryant. His spirit continues to assist in the transformation of so many lives and is still only a stone's throw away.